DESIGNING THE MODERN WORLD LANGUAGE CLASSROOM

How to Guide Students to Proficiency

DESIGNING THE MODERN WORLD LANGUAGE CLASSROOM

How to Guide Students to Proficiency

MEGAN GOLDEN

Tandem Light Press
950 Herrington Rd.
Suite C128
Lawrenceville, GA 30044

Tandem Light Press paperback edition Winter 2021

ISBN: ISBN 979-8-9856404-0-3

Library of Congress Control Number:

PRINTED IN THE UNITED STATES OF AMERICA

CONTENTS

FOREWORD

MY NAME IS Dr. Steve McCammon, and I am the President and Chief Executive Officer of the Schlechty Center located in Louisville, Kentucky. More importantly, perhaps, is that I was a school superintendent for many years, and I was a fierce advocate for the notion that a focus on student engagement is central to the pursuit of profound learning for all students. I do believe that my commitment to that, as well as the role that I have been given to help carry on the work of Dr. Phillip Schlechty, noted author and founder of the Schlechty Center, is the reason that I have been honored to write a foreword to this important work by Megan Golden (née King).

We at the Schlechty Center have come to know and develop a great respect for Megan as a gifted teacher who truly has a belief system that all students bring a motivation to learn into the classroom. We share her deep commitment and belief that it is the role of the teacher to become a leader and designer of engaging work for the students in their care. We share her belief, as you will see detailed in her work, that while all students bring a motivation to learn, it is our role as educators to seek out those motivations and to design work that will meet those motivations to deepen students' engagement in the good work that we want them to know and be able to do.

Dr. Schlechty often observed that "schools have become a place where kids come to watch adults work." As a lifelong learner and educator, I see how in many cases this has become true, and that a fundamental shift in how we think about teaching and learning is needed. At the heart of this change is the very notion of the teacher becoming more of a leader of engagement and a designer for learning. What Megan Golden has written here is a very practical approach to understanding this shift and how world language teachers can reconceive the work their students do. While her focus is on designing engaging work in the world language classroom, what she shares in this new book transfers across all content and learning environments for sure. This book is about quality teaching and learning with deep care for students and the voice that they bring to their own learning.

I am eager for teacher leaders, and those who support and build the capacity for those teachers to excel, to enjoy this new book. It is my experience that so much professional learning today, and books written about teacher improvement, are very program oriented. What Megan captures here is the value of creating a common language around design and applying it to how teachers assess student motivation, honor student voice, and design lessons that appeal to student motives. So many times, we hear educators talk about how professional learning can feel like an extra burden on an already overwhelming sea of changes in the field. What Megan describes in this book is one teacher's journey in cutting through some of that dense noise to focus on how to truly achieve impact by getting very clear about what the students need and how being thoughtful in a quality design process can achieve that desired goal.

I agreed to write this foreword because I believe deeply in the work that Megan has put forth in her new book. If you are a teacher, what you will get out of this book is a new way to consider how you can better connect with your students by considering the motivations they bring to the work. You will also come to understand the power of creating a common language around the Schlechty Center's Design Qualities that will serve you in your design thinking and will encourage important collaboration with your colleagues. If you are a principal or district leader, you will come to understand the power of building the capacity for your staff to focus on becoming teacher leaders and to use design thinking in deepening the engagement of all students. Moreover, she has laid out in detail some specific ways to make that important goal a reality in the classroom of today.

It was time for this book to be written. Dr. Schlechty wrote a series of important works in his lifetime. One of his most widely read books was Engaging Students: The Next Level of Working on the Work (2011). In that book, he wrote about the importance of understanding student engagement and how educators can increase the opportunity to maximize it by considering the use of Design Qualities to create an appeal to those very student motivations that students bring to the classroom. What Megan has done in this book is to take that work to a practical level and share how this can work in the world language classroom and beyond. Dr. Schlechty would be a proud and avid consumer of this work. I know that I am as well.

Dr. Steve McCammon
President and CEO of the Schlechty Center

Why You Need Design in your World Language Classroom

THINK ABOUT THE last time you flew a paper airplane. Did you have a plan for folding the paper? Did you make any measurements or follow a template? Once folded, did you fly the plane from there, or did you move somewhere better for flying? How well did it fly? Did it survive to make a second flight?

The way you design and fold your plane determines how high, how far, and what direction the plane flies. After the flight, you probably assessed your work. Maybe you made some modifications to that plane, or maybe you scrapped it for a different design altogether. Maybe you had to account for an obstacle or a breeze that pulled your flight off course. Just folding the plane wasn't enough. Your design had an important purpose: flight! And even the most inspired design is only as valuable as its performance.

Ultimately, our flight trajectory depends on what we know about folds and flight, what choices we make for our context, and how we assess, reflect on, and improve our work. Like your paper airplane, your students' learning depends on your design. We study pedagogy and get to know our students. We make adjustments for classroom and community contexts or personal obstacles. We assess performance and tailor action steps accordingly. And if everything comes together, learning lifts off and student achievement soars.

Envisioning teaching as a process of design captures the elements that affect our outcome. It's not just methodology. It's not just research. It's not just student demographics. Instructional design is a craft built through knowledge, action, and reflection. I was introduced to the philosophy of design as a participant in the Professional Association of Georgia Educators (PAGE)'s Teacher Academy, led by team members from the Schlechty Center. The Schlechty Center's philosophy on teaching and learning, primarily embodied in Working on the Work (WOW), but also in their philosophy on schools and systems, speaks to me on a deep level in a way that no other course has. It connects my academic learning to professional experience so that I can see a broad view of my role as a teacher. In addition to the primary implications it has had on my work in the classroom, it has opened my eyes to my work in the world, and thereby extended the role of my students 'from students in my room' to 'my students in the world.' It is liberating, it is powerful, and it is visionary.

The philosophy of design builds my fundamental understanding of student work and learning. Whereas other teacher resources may promote research data as the answer to a classroom issue, or instructional methodology for achieving certain results, the philosophy of design focuses on the student's interaction with work as the key to learning. Student success relies on the teacher's understanding of individual learners' needs and preferences. The teacher's role becomes much more nurturing in this sense, designing situations for learning which motivate students to pursue content. The teacher's role as source and assessor of standards is minimized in favor of that of a facilitator who cultivates learning opportunities of inherent value to students. While our systems dictate local, state, or federal standards for which teachers and students must demonstrate compliance and mastery, reality dictates that individuals pursue learning experiences that have personal meaning. By designing engaging work tailored to students' lives, but which still results in content mastery, we create conditions for students to personally connect with language learning.

The longer I studied the Schlechty Center's principles of design, the more I sought to connect with other language teachers who were making or had made the transformation that I was experiencing. I wanted to find teachers who modeled the philosophy of design. While I found some world language teachers whose practices reflected what I studied, and I had a teacher network in the Academy of new Schlechty Center apprentices, I failed to find others who identified both as world language teachers and WOW designers. Many colleagues were committed to designing engaging learning experiences but continued to focus on their classroom instruction, rather than their students' participation in learning as global citizens. This book is a product of my passion to help colleagues in world language education understand the philosophy of design.

The premise underlying the Schlechty Center's philosophy on work is that qualities built into design affect a person's engagement in their work. Within the context of the classroom, these design qualities, coupled with measures of engagement and effective assessment, constitute what the Center calls the "Classroom Standards." In their statement *Schlechty Center on Engagement*, a student is considered engaged when:

- The student sees the activity as personally meaningful;
- The student's level of interest is sufficiently high that he persists in the face of difficulty;
- The student finds the task sufficiently challenging that she believes she will accomplish something of worth by doing it; and
- The student's emphasis is on optimum performance and on "getting it right."[1]

As a teacher and student of modern language, this philosophy of engagement is true to my own experiences. As a high school student, I was motivated to study Spanish because of the large number of Spanish-speaking students with whom I attended school. Despite any difficulty I may have had in the classroom, and the difficulty I remember having trying to communicate with my Spanish-speaking friends, I persisted, year after year, so that I could master the language. The benefits I stood to gain by doing so included being a better friend, traveling the world, and getting a competitive edge in the job market.

Now, after more than a decade in the classroom, as I strive to design in a way that engages my students in learning and results in mastery of language, I find myself digging into those very same factors that affected my own engagement. I have to get to know my students and design language tasks with results they value. I have to minimize the level of risk and difficulty my students will inevitably face as novices trying to function in real-time and real-life communication so that they will persist even though they realize their lack of competence. I have to organize learning and present clear standards so that my students can set and reach goals for success.

Though the research on language learning and acquisition is plentiful,

---

1   *Schlechty Center On Engagement*. 1st ed. Schlechty Center, 2015. Web. 12 May 2015.

and the literature on teaching methods exhaustive, I was dissatisfied with the absence of a holistic approach to the method that remained relevant and effective no matter what the predominant "best practice" of the day might be and regardless of the background of my students. I have long felt that many of the methods I had studied and practiced, while great for an enthusiastic learner who had potential access to world travel and language speakers, failed to take in the reality of today's standardized classrooms and the fact the majority of US world language students are extremely unlikely to engage in world travel or to participate in daily conversation with others who speak their language of study. Let's check out a few facts to this point:

- The US Census Bureau reports that 79.3% of US residents speak only English[2];
- When TheExpeditioner.com compared State Department statistics from 2013 with census data, he found that about two in five Americans have a passport[3];
- In economic terms, 40% of households earn less than $50,000 per year[4]; and
- The National Center for Education Statistics (2020) reports that approximately 18% of U.S. school-age children live in poverty, and, among families of color, the rate climbs as high as 32%[5].

These statistics paint the picture of a classroom filled with mostly English-speaking, low to middle-class students, the majority of whom will not leave the country. On top of the barriers already posed by poverty to our low-income students, the Center for Applied Linguistics found that modern language courses "were offered in smaller percentages of rural schools and

2   U.S. Census Bureau. (2013). *Selected social characteristics in the United States.* Retrieved May 12, 2015 from http://www.factfinder.census.gov.

3   Stabile, M. (2016, Dec 11). *How Many Americans Have a Passport?* The Expeditioner. www.theexpeditioner.com/wordpress/2010/02/17/how-many-americans-have-a-passport-2/.

4   United States Census Bureau. *Selected economic characteristics: 2019 ACSurvey 5-year estimates data profiles.* Retrieved May 6, 2021 from data.census.gov.

5   Institute of Education Sciences: National Center for Education Statistics. (2020). *The Condition of Education - Characteristics of Children's Families.* Retrieved May 7, 2021 from Nces.ed.gov.

schools whose students were from lower socioeconomic backgrounds"[6]. However, it is precisely those students from poor or rural backgrounds, put at the greatest distance from world language, who stand to reap the greatest practical benefit from language skills in the workplace. Even Forbes pointed out the benefits of learning more languages when it referenced research by Saiz and Zoido (2005) showing a nearly 4% wage increase for employees that spoke more than one language[7,8]. World language teachers are poised to provide some of the most relevant global learning available in a school setting. World language proficiency and cultural competence gives students of all backgrounds practical skills and a competitive edge as job seekers.

Given the rapid development of global communications and business, the study of world languages is integral to developing students who have competence interacting with speakers of other languages, and who are sensitive to unfamiliar cultural practices and traditions. Allow me to share two examples from my own classroom. I taught a high school junior in first-year Spanish. His family had immigrated from Southwest Asia in his youth and English was his second language. He performed fantastically in our early units on numbers, calendars, and small talk, many times sounding like a native speaker. Through our conversations, I learned that his family-owned two local restaurants and that many of the staff were Hispanic. Since he was one of two sons that helped run the restaurant over a period of several years, he had developed language skills for managing and getting along with employees at his family's business. Consequently, for units like health and wellness that didn't have a strong connection to his workplace, he struggled to develop proficiency at the same level. In another case, I struggled with a first-year sophomore who was constantly distracted by his phone. When I had an opportunity to discuss this conflict of interest with him, I learned that he had been designing simple video game apps and marketing them. His grandfather had promised to match his earnings to help purchase his first car. He was constantly monitoring, improving, and designing apps to

---

6   Rhodes, N., & Pufahl, I. (2009) *Foreign Language Teaching in U.S. Schools: Results of a National Survey*. [Executive Summary]. Center for Applied Linguistics.

7   Conner, C. (2014, April 17). How Learning an Additional Language Could Influence Your Business. *Forbes*. N.p. Retrieved June 21, 2015.

8   Saiz, A. & Zoido, E. (2005). "Listening to What the World Says: Bilingualism and Earnings in the United States." *The Review of Economics and Statistics, 87*(3), p. 523-538.

that end. He even told me that he was working on making the apps available in Spanish to broaden his clientele and increase his earnings. As is the case in my examples, all of the students sitting in our classrooms can connect to our language of study. It takes personal conversations to discover how we can use these connections to make language study personally relevant and meaningful on a day-to-day basis.

Any of our students may be the next entrepreneur to develop and market a product, potentially developing it into a global business. Without language skills and cultural competence, businesses cannot pursue and maintain success. Local businesses, particularly in metropolitan areas and farming communities, may find themselves serving or employing growing immigrant or refugee communities. Towns compete to attract international business developers looking to build factories and extend their reach with warehouses and training facilities. If communities and businesses stand by the philosophy of "We speak English here," they limit their potential client base and create an exclusionary, toxic attitude that cannot further the vision of any company that seeks to sustain itself. As former Program Specialist, Jon Valentine stated eloquently for the Georgia Department of Education (GADOE):

> Regional expertise, cross-cultural competence, and advanced language proficiency are… skills that will enhance any career field, encourage international investment to our state, and develop a workforce that is successful in working on diverse international teams to collaborate and solve global problems. Developing international perspective and advanced language proficiency… will ensure our nation's security and will support our statewide and regional economic development goals [while providing] a competitive advantage that moves an applicant's resume to the top of the pile.[9]

It is precisely this competitive advantage that we stand to offer today's students. We must develop language programs that drive students toward advanced proficiency and give students a contemporary understanding of what it means to interact with people from other cultures and regions.

---

9   Valentine, Jon. *World Languages and Global/Workforce Initiatives.* GADOE Curriculum and Instruction, n.d. Web. Retrieved 10 June 2013.

The biggest job of a world language teacher is to empower her students to see themselves as players and participants in our global economy. Teachers must design work for their students which has inherent, tangible, and unquestionable value. The study of world language must cultivate an awareness in our students that knowing people, interacting with people, and being a good communicator are equally as valuable, if not more valuable, than technical skills like nursing, engineering, or farming. The work that we design must build our students' learning from the inside out, with its foundation lying in the needs, experiences, and goals that our students already have. If we truly want to engage our students and to launch them into a world that already understands the importance of being able to work with a global vision, we must bring the content to them in personally meaningful ways.

In this book, I plan to walk you through a fresh look at world language education through the lens of the Schlechty Center's Classroom Standards. My goals are for you to:

- understand the work you design as a reflection of the design qualities that affect your students;
- measure your students' engagement and implement systems for reflection and redesign;
- craft work—formative and summative assessments—that has personal meaning to each of your students, and which also result in language mastery; and
- develop a hunger within you and your students to find power in language.

This book is organized according to the design qualities and standards. Because they are interrelated, you will inevitably notice common ground between them. Beyond developing your understanding of Working on the Work, I will give you practical examples, tools, and resources to get you started on design!

An Introduction to the Classroom
Standards & Some Assumptions

NOW THAT WE'VE established the importance of the Philosophy of Design and its relevance to the world language classroom, I'd like to give you a "primer" to review some of the basic tenets of Working on the Work. The chapters that follow will help you dive deep into the design qualities and understand how they may appear in your classroom, but their foundation comes from Phil Schlechty's *Working on the Work* (2002) and *Engaging Students* (2011). For readers that may not have a background in Schlechty's work, we will start with some basic understandings and assumptions. The first is what the Schlechty Center terms the "Classroom Standards," which encompass the ten design qualities of work, along with engagement and assessment. We introduced engagement in the first chapter, and for now, I will define "assessment" simply as evaluation of progress towards goals. Below, in brief, are the design qualities. No single design quality holds more weight or importance than another, and the order that I have listed them is simply the order in which I happened to write them.

- Protection from Adverse Consequences: Work without fear of punishment, embarrassment, or inadequacy
- Authenticity: Work satisfies the authentic purposes, needs, and desires of the students
- Choice: Students have some level of control over the work they are doing
- Product Focus: Work results in a product or performance
- Clear and Compelling Standards: Students understand what they are expected to know and do
- Content and Substance: High-quality intellectual work, rich and profound knowledge

- Organization of Knowledge: Knowledge is clear and accessible by nature of the way it is presented or discovered
- Affirmation: "Significant others" affirm your work
- Affiliation: Interdependent, collaborative work
- Novelty and Variety: New forms of work and new products

Working on the Work posits that these qualities are interwoven to varying degrees in the work that you design for your students. Some tasks may satisfy multiple qualities, others may connect to just a few. These qualities will appeal differently to different students, but the goal is to design tasks in a way that incorporates the design qualities that engage most of your students most of the time. By the same token, if your students are not engaged, you have not designed engaging work. It is also important to note that engagement alone does not equal content mastery. For example, Fiesta Friday registers very high levels of engagement but doesn't add much in the way of structural fluency. Our goals are both engagement and communicative growth.

We will also assume that students can learn. They learn constantly, just not always about the content we wish them to learn. Information is merely a YouTube video or Wikipedia page away, so it will also be assumed that students are capable of finding information. As a teacher, your business is to model how the information and skills of your content area can improve the lives of your students, and you must be capable of designing learning experiences and giving feedback that helps them advance and perfect their knowledge and skill.

Let's say your students want to know about gaming in the target language. They have background knowledge of how the game works. They can find their way to the gaming community of target language speakers. They can use translators and dictionaries to interpret the things that are said to them and communicate basic information to other gamers. Why do they need a teacher? Will any of this independent work be valued or contribute to their classroom success? In many classrooms, the answer is no. Those words aren't on vocabulary lists. Spending an hour navigating the game's landscape following game, gamer, and tutorial instructions in the target language won't fill in any blanks on their test. But this is authentic study and use. It holds value in the world, and consequently to your students. You must figure out how your class will build skills and proficiency for students like these because these are the students in your room. They don't need the answers. They need the practice, the work, and your expert feedback for improvement.

Dominant research—and common understanding of second language learning—supports that the more you hear and attempt a language, the more quickly you learn to use it. Many teachers interpret this to mean that if they do everything in the target language at a level at which students can understand, students will move towards proficiency. Comprehensible input becomes a full-time performance for the teacher involving props, Power-Points, Total Physical Response (TPR), scripted guides, etc. This line of thinking puts the teacher completely in charge of the transmission of information and makes the students totally reliant on the teacher for learning. It also makes the teacher totally and completely exhausted. It's no wonder some teachers abandon ACTFL's goal that 90% of class time be spent in the target language[10].

The responsibility does not lie entirely on the teacher to be the source and manager of language. Students are your "knowledge workers." Give them the resources, guided tasks, and inspiration and they will find and organize knowledge of the target language using the target language. For example, in a sports unit, many teachers would introduce the unit with fancy pictures on a SmartBoard or PowerPoint, or maybe with printed pictures and props. Next, the teacher might model motions to represent the necessary vocabulary about sports—games, equipment, places, players. In this example, information is cultivated by the teacher and transmitted to students through the direct instruction and modeling of the teacher. Students may spend most of their time listening to and perhaps responding with the target language, but most production that is to be done will be driven by the teacher.

A student-work-centered approach to this unit may be to model and provide the names of several sports (many of which may be cognates). Next, direct students to realia (authentic sources from the "real" world) that pertains to their sport: ESPN in the target language, sporting goods store advertisements, stadium websites. Ask students to get in groups by preferred sport and to prepare to present the top 10 critical words for their sport to

10   American Council on the Teaching of Foreign Languages. (2010, May 22). *ACTFL Position Statement: Use of the Target Language in the Classroom.* Retrieved May 2, 2017 from https://www.actfl.org/news/position-statements/use-the-target-language-the-classroom.

the class. They can find the information. The process will use resources that are authentic to the students. The result will be relevant to their interests because they select it. To complete the work, they must work interdependently to delegate research and create a team product. They can choose who they work with, what sport they'll study, and the words that they deem most important to authentic language use. As the expert, you will give them feedback and guidance as to the words they select, and then you will help them organize their knowledge when they come back together as a class to share their respective vocabulary. Meanwhile, you, the teacher, don't have to do any song and dance to keep their attention. They still spend most of the class time invested in interpreting and producing the target language. The activity is novel to this unit of study. You still achieve engagement and content mastery, and students respect you more in the morning because you gave them choice and honored their interests and abilities.

If you've ever organized a service project, you know that your success at getting volunteers to help will be driven by the reasons people volunteer to participate. Does the cause have personal meaning to them? Will the participant get some benefit, such as service hours for a scholarship? Do people volunteer so that they can spend time with their friends or be part of a team? Once the project begins, if your volunteers aren't getting the work done, it does no good to threaten or punish them because you run the risk that they won't do any more work at all. Instead, you find ways to re-engage them that will result in their wanting to get the job done. Unlike a service project, it is often the case that students don't volunteer to be part of a classroom—more often they are assigned to it. They do, however, arrive as volunteers to class work. When students don't engage in the work, they don't master the content. If we punish them with grades or threaten them with disciplinary consequences, we run the risk that they will choose not to engage in future work. If a teacher's true objective is to successfully help all students learn, he has an obligation to design work that all students will volunteer for.

The ten design qualities introduced at the start of this chapter are the keys to creating learning experiences that students volunteer for. In the chapters which follow, we will take a closer look at the meaning and significance of each quality and consider how strategies for modern language learning affect design for engagement.

Big Ideas

In this chapter, we previewed the design qualities and discussed some key assumptions that lay the foundation for the Philosophy of Design. Those assumptions are:

1. Students can learn.
2. Students are capable of finding information.
3. Students are knowledge workers.
4. Students are volunteers to the work.

Questions for Reflection

1. What design quality or qualities do you feel confident that you have background experience with? Which one(s) are you curious about?
2. How have you seen your students learn and find information on their own? What kinds of topics and learning activities do they pursue? In what formats do they engage in learning (internet search, personally with a coach, experimentation, books in the library, social media query, etc.)?
3. What is a task you have tried that you would like to see your students do more of the work than you? What changes could you make for that to happen?
4. What are some things you already do that students "volunteer" for? Why do you think these activities are so engaging for them?

PROTECTION FROM ADVERSE CONSEQUENCES FOR INITIAL FAILURES

Work without fear of punishment, embarrassment, or inadequacy

FOR A BEGINNING student of language, nothing is felt more keenly than failure—mispronouncing words, not knowing how to spell, not understanding what is being said, not knowing what to say. Students, especially high school students, may be uncomfortable or easily frustrated because simple tasks, like spelling their name or asking to go to the bathroom, suddenly become risky in an unfamiliar language. "What if I don't say it right? What if the teacher doesn't understand, or if I don't understand the teacher? What if my friends laugh at me?" Students who can write essays and read novels suddenly struggle to use a verb or read simple sentences. Without proper support, students become afraid, guarded, reluctant.

"Protection from adverse consequences for initial failures" means that as a teacher develops knowledge in her students, she integrates formative tasks and assessments to give students feedback that helps them grow towards proficiency. Once they've had the opportunity to experiment, learn, and master the skill, they are asked to demonstrate mastery in summative assessments. In other words, a student is "safe," shielded from failure, and first given the resources and opportunities to try a new skill and master it before he is asked to "prove it." In a chemistry class, for example, a student learning about chemical reactions will work through the equations and reactions with many practice questions or scenarios before the teacher hands over the chemicals and beakers. Once students have had feedback and practice, they are assessed to ascertain their mastery of the objective, and either advanced or remediated based on the outcome.

Although protection from failing grades is relatively easy for a teacher to guarantee through proactive planning, creating an environment where initial failure is embraced as a tool for growth is harder to ensure. It's easy for a student to risk himself with pencil and paper. Nobody else can hear what he's calculated. In language learning, however, students must verbalize their trials with every objective. They speak to the teacher, they converse with peers, they present to the class. Their feedback is immediate because either they will understand and be understood, or they won't. For students who are afraid of failure, speaking is a risk. For students who prefer a pencil to a partner, speaking is a risk. For students who have little exposure to world languages, or whose families are ignorant of world cultures and speakers of other languages, delving into the world of the "others" is a risk.

All of these levels of risk pose a critical challenge to engagement in world language study. The second indicator for engagement is that "the student's level of interest is sufficiently high that he persists in the face of difficulty." So, two things have to happen. First, we have to pique the student's level of interest. Second, we have to create an environment that diminishes risk, and in which students trust deep in their hearts that the teacher and their peers will not judge them as failures as they attempt to use language.

While teachers understand how to moderate their comments to encourage participation, beginning students who have never been in a world language classroom may not have the understanding or vocabulary to encourage their peers. It is essential that the teacher models with enthusiasm that any participation is good participation. Otherwise, the teacher will be talking to herself most of the class period.

If you're uncertain where to start with low-risk activities, the following are quick and easy tools to get students volunteering to speak. These activities get students speaking quickly, need a minimal amount of preparation, and provide tangible evidence for assessment. These tried-and-true ideas for speaking activities are designed to be low-risk and high-interest. I have included samples of these materials in English, but would, of course, be presenting them in the target language for classroom use.

Reducing Risk in Speaking Activities

Popsicle Stick Participation

One of the fastest and most efficient ways to get students to participate is to put something in their hands that represents their participation. What a morale boost to see students straining so hard to get their hands highest that they've nearly come out of their seats, and then whine and beg when it's time to move on to another activity. You could use any token to get their attention, but I prefer to use popsicle sticks because I can use them again, they're harder to get into trouble with or break, and they're cheap to replace. However, you could use straws, sticky notes, crayons, pirate tokens, playing cards, dried beans, or whatever else you happen to have on hand. This speaking activity is particularly useful for reinforcing vocabulary or verb tenses.

How to do it:

A. **Show your class a picture prompt on the topic of study**. In our weather unit, I have a PowerPoint with several slides with different weather scenes. In our shopping unit, I use a crowded picture of shoppers bursting through the doors for holiday sales.

B. **Ask students to tell you about what they see**. Anything in the target language is fair game, no matter how simple or complex, obvious or obscure. For novice or nervous speakers, you may want to allow them to name and describe nouns, or for higher-level or braver speakers, you may specify that their contribution must be a sentence or use a particular verb tense. You may want to require that only original contributions will be awarded points.

C. **Every time a student volunteers, hand him a popsicle stick**. Explain that students will receive points based on the number of times they participate. Don't distinguish between simple and complex answers with points because getting your low-level speakers to share anything is equally as monumental as getting your high-level speakers to make compound sentences with advanced verb forms. If your low-level speaker pulls off a complex sentence, then you may want to think about extra points to celebrate!

D. Record the points however you like. They can be class participation points, a bonus on a quiz, etc. If you make this activity a regular one, you can set a goal for the number of sticks to collect to make or exceed the grade for the day. There will always be students who are excited to have an opportunity to exceed.

Sample Record of Popsicle Points

Name	9/21 (school unit)	10/24 (leisure time)	Particip. Pts.
Amanda	/ /	/ / /	5
Beto	/ / / /	/ / / /	8
Carla	/	/	2

Another good reason to have a visual token of participation is that it allows the teacher to target those students who are hesitant to speak. When everyone is excited to share, and you take the time to invite those students who never speak to share in the excitement, they grow in the esteem of their peers. It is up to you to wait, to encourage, and to prompt them; to tell the others, "No, you will wait because I want to hear her voice too. I know she has something to share." Based on the data from the activity chart above, it would be easy for a teacher to assess that Carla perceives risk and either needs skill support or confidence building so that she can perform in a range similar to her peers. Since students can easily earn at least two points per instance, it would be good to suggest the next time you play, that a goal of three points earned would be a "good" range. Some will be eager to exceed the goal, some will be satisfied with "good," and setting a target will up the ante if stragglers have been content with one or two points.

Guided Conversations with Choice

For students or groups that struggle with risk, or with novice learners who need more support, a great confidence booster is a guided conversation with choice. Many pair speaking activities tend to give students all the information, or none of the information. For example, "Have Giselle read Student A's script, and Francois read Student B's script;" or "Pretend you're ordering food. Have one student speak as the waiter, and the other speak as the patron." In the scripted example, student individuality is completely lacking. There is little relevance, or authenticity, to reading someone else's conversation out loud. Further, the task makes a partner irrelevant. Though the script has two people, your two students will not actually be doing anything one student couldn't do by himself. While some students will enjoy the opportunity to be affirmed by how good they sound, students who don't seek affirmation (or who know they don't sound good) may be put off by this lack of choice. In the "pretend" example, students who may not have mastered the material will be at great risk because the prompt lacks scaffolding or support for a struggling learner. It will be difficult to engage a student who fears failure and has no support. There is no way for him to even comply with what you've asked him to do, and not complying, in addition to failure, may land him in trouble for disobedience. A good alternative is to give students a guided conversation, but one in which they have an opportunity to make choices about what they say. This supports the struggling or fearful learner, makes accomplishing the task a job that will require interdependence, and adds novelty and choice. Here's an example about travel:

Speak to three classmates about your travels, real or imagined. Read the sentence below, choosing words to make your sentence complete. Record information about your partners by marking their first initial by their responses.

In the		I travel to the		to see	
	Spring		lake		animals
	Summer		mountains		my family
	Fall		desert		nature
	Winter		woods		

Sample Table for Guided Conversation with Choice

After students record the data from their guided conversations, you could extend the activity into a presentational writing or speaking activity in which they draw conclusions based on what they and their peers indicated about their travels. For example, "In the winter, Suzette and Gerard travel to the mountains to see family."

Creative Partnering
While always working with the same partner is safe, it doesn't always create the best pairing for learning, it doesn't allow students to listen to a variety of speakers, and it doesn't give students the necessary reminder that they all have different abilities and strengths and that's OK! For quick, "tell your neighbor"-type activities, working with a favorite classmate is fine, but for more formalized speaking work, it helps to have some prepared strategies for mixing and mingling your students. Some of my favorite pairing strategies include:

A. **Time Partners:** Find a clock, or a map, or a body parts chart — something with easily identifiable pieces that students will know or study during their time will you. Have them fill in a different partner for each piece of their chart. (Hannah and Beth are each other's 1 o'clock, Ed and Robby are each other's 2 o'clock, etc.) Next time you need a partner who's not their neighbor, direct them to the partner they filled in. "Find your 3 o'clock partner."

B. **No neighbors:** You may not work with anyone seated within one seat of you, or from the same row, or section as you, or whose desks touch your desk (depending on your seating arrangement), etc.

C. **SWAP:** Your partners must come from the opposite half of the room. (Side A student must work with Side B student) Also, if different roles are involved, you can divide them by the side of the room students come from. For example, you can work with anyone, but the person whose seat is closest to the door will be the nurse, and the person whose seat is closest to the window will be the patient.

D. **Cup O' Numbers:** Have students pull a numbered popsicle stick from a cup. Your partner(s) have the same number as you. Depending on the size of your group, you can also do this with playing cards. If you need small groups, you could group them with colored stickers as they enter.

E. **Speed-dating:** For guided improvisational speaking, seat students as if they were speed-dating. Display a timer and a prompt and ask students to discuss the prompt, or at least use it as a starting point for a conversation with that partner that lasts until the timer chimes. Then, move on to a new partner and new topic. Before the start of the activity, brainstorm some ways to keep a conversation going if students don't know what else to say.

A Word on Language Labs

Classroom access to language learning technology is widely varied. In my classroom, my language lab is the best no-risk tool I have. From my work-station, I can pair students over headsets randomly or manually, and, best of all, students have no knowledge of which students their classmates are paired with! Students who would never work with each other, or the students who nobody wants to work with, can suddenly get their work done without drama or discussion because nobody else knows, partners are randomly selected, and partners only last for the duration of an activity. I am able to hear the voices of students who would never share in front of the class, or even with peers, and most importantly, their peers hear their voices. They are valuable and necessary for doing the work which needs to be done.

Modeling Success & Honoring Student Voice

Part of reducing risk is to make your expectations clear and model what success looks like so that your students have a chance to achieve it. Using a task or proficiency rubric gives students clear, attainable steps for assessing their abilities and developing their skills. Giving students the tools for self-assessment, and assessing students with the same tool, is a good way to lower risk. On a simple scale, we do this with study guides. "Can you complete the sentence with the verb form? Can you write a short answer to the question?" However, if you want to get students thinking critically about their real-world proficiency, and not just their ability to get the blanks right, it is necessary to use a tool that lays out clear steps for growth and that students and teachers alike can turn to for feedback. We'll talk about this more when we discuss Assessment.

Throughout this chapter, we have identified factors that affect a student's risk in the world languages classroom. We looked at models for designing low-risk formative presentational and interpersonal speaking assessments. We have discussed some factors that affect risk, like clear and compelling product standards, product focus, affiliation, and affirmation. I would stress, though, that the number one way to lower risk is through the environment you nurture in your classroom. Giving students a voice is powerful! For it to happen for your students, you must lay the foundation and expectations that:

- everyone's voice counts;
- all target language use is good target language use (and nobody better tell you otherwise); and
- the teacher cares enough to follow up (counting participation points and calling on the stragglers, making sure everybody gets to work with a partner who gives them a voice).

When you model and enforce these expectations, you create an environment where students are fearless in their learning, and in which they expect their classmates to be free from fear as well. Particularly for students who have been silenced or had their voice discounted, perhaps because of race, gender, or sexual identity, it is essential that the teacher intentionally make space for marginalized voices who may be particularly fearful of the consequences of speaking up in front of peers or teachers. If you are really going to create an environment where everyone's voice counts, you have to ensure that everyone has a voice. When students engage in behaviors that silence their peers, it is your responsibility to hold them accountable and reinforce your expectation that each student will be heard and be responded to with dignity. It fills me with pride to overhear a student encouraging another to speak in my classroom because it means they believe in themselves too when they tell their partners, "It's ok if you make a mistake, they're just words." "Mistakes are how we learn. If you don't try the task now, you won't be ready for the assessment later." "Nobody cares how you sound because we're all beginners, so we're supposed to sound like this."

BIG IDEAS

Protection from adverse consequences for initial failures means that students engage in work without fear of punishment, embarrassment, or inadequacy. To accomplish this, we have to (1) design engaging work, and (2) diminish fear. We can shield students from fear with superficial steps such as how we weight grades, but more importantly, we have to build an environment where failure is embraced as a tool for growth. Teachers can reduce risk for students by building trusting classroom relationships that honor student voice and implementing activities like Popsicle Stick Participation, Guided Conversations with Choice, or Creative Partnering that help ensure all students can be heard.

Questions for Reflection

1. Think of a time when a teacher punished or embarrassed you. Even though a long time has passed, your feelings may still be strong. Do you remember what you were learning that day? How did the teacher's action affect your work after that moment? If our goal is student engagement, what does this memory teach you about how your behavior can impact students?

2. Resilience is a person's ability to recover from setbacks or challenges. If you build a classroom environment where failure is embraced as a tool for growth, how can students transfer these skills and mindsets to other contexts?

3. If students can get away with mocking or belittling their peers, how does that affect students' level of risk in a classroom, and, subsequently, classroom engagement?

4. From the sample activities suggested, what is one that you would like to try? How would you adapt it to your context?

AUTHENTICITY

Work satisfies the authentic purposes, needs, and desires of the student

IN THE REALM of world language instruction, when we speak of authenticity, what we're often talking about is realia, or learning materials that are artifacts of life in the target language. While realia is intensely important, simply using it does not necessarily result in engagement. To bring you back to the four indicators of engagement, the first states that in order for a student to be engaged, he must, "[see] the activity as personally meaningful." When it comes to engaging students in language, authenticity means that the work must connect with students' authentic needs for language use and that it must connect in meaningful authentic ways with students because it incorporates their interests, results in a product that holds meaning or results in affirmation for them, or which honors their learning style through the mode in which the work takes place.

DESIGN FOR STUDENTS' NEEDS

The work you design for students must speak to the students' needs for language use. In other words, the language you're trying to teach your students must be language that suits their purposes. For example, if you teach affluent, college-bound students, they may want to learn the target language for relatively immediate social and college goals (spring break in Cancun, volunteering with speakers of other languages at their mom's office, studying abroad in France, exempting college foreign language requirements). However, if you teach world languages at a career academy, your students may be driven by community communication that suits their work prospects (customer service at the shop, marketing to potential foreign buyers, direct-ing the kitchen staff as a chef). I don't mean to overgeneralize your students, but to point out that you will be the one to know these kinds of things about the learners in your room and it will be up to you to design work and uti-lize resources that speak to their authentic needs. Now, while your job is to design learning situations that encourage their development of knowledge, you still have to design student need-driven work that gets your students to mastery of your content standards.

So, let's say the teacher's need (standard) is to get students to be able to talk about family relationships in the target language. Let's say many of her students come from diverse families: they have a single parent or step-family, they have family members who are incarcerated, they don't know certain branches of their family tree. To fit their families into the neat little oversimplified tree charts and talk about husbands and wives and give details like full names, ages, occupations, and origins is rather absurd, and often uncomfortable. For our conversation about family to be authentic to stu-dents, the teacher has to pick a family that comes from their world. We could go with pop culture and chart a well-known family like the Kardashians or the Simpsons. We could go with politics and chart families of current politi-cal leaders like the royal family of Spain, or the family of the president of Mexico. I have to speak my target language through the cultural language of my students' world! I have to connect with them in ways where they seek to connect, like with pop media and current events. My students are already talking about the Kardashians and learning about world politics and history, I just have to give them the tools to do so in the target language. Further, by ensuring that we select materials that represent diverse families, we help create classroom environments that welcome diversity and give students the language to express life in their own terms.

The pot of "authenticity" gold is realia which targets student needs in meaningful ways. If you're addressing your students' professional goals, start by using materials from their industries that are in the target language. Hand-books, guides, fliers, advertisements, and websites for mainstream professions are easy to find on the web in other languages. If I were giving a unit on directions and addresses, a quick target language search of some keywords like "Mechanic Service Pamphlet" will likely land you with some realia that suits the needs of the topic. Sometimes a little extra digging will also get you to appropriate realia. For example, in a unit on grooming and hygiene, browsing digital fashion magazines (or maybe you can afford subscriptions to hard copies) will often turn up advertisements for current brand name beauty products. Students' background knowledge of those products will make the content more accessible and authentic. Your students will appreciate that you personalized your content in a way that is relevant to their moment with you. By accessing connections that students already have, you open doors for learning more quickly and build a relationship with your students that's founded on respect because you take the time to honor them in the work you design. Also, by connecting language to products perhaps already in their homes, students realize that target language speakers are like them too, and they can begin to see others as more like themselves.

In addition to resources that are authentic to your students' lives, it is important to make sure that your objectives are authentic to their needs as well. While grammar and structure are necessary elements of communication, your students will want to know what they can walk away today and do. When they leave your room today, what will they say when asked, "What did you do today? What did you learn today?" If their answer is "Copy the verb forms and learn how to conjugate," then they haven't learned how to *do* with language. Their answer should be more along the lines of "We talked about what we do after school. I learned how to use verbs to tell what my friends and I do." Design your work around the proficiencies and not around the grammar and vocabulary points. Students in any year of study may be able to conjugate a verb, but how they use them to provide information or explain an event will distinguish their ability and allow the teacher to give targeted feedback that will lead the student to advance in proficiency.

You do your students an injustice if you simply count your days in vocabulary and structure topics. Likewise, you can assess cultural trivia, or you can seek out holistic synthesis of cultural practices, perspectives, and products so that students can make connections between their lives and the lives of native speakers. Your job is to give students the authentic benefit of developing language and cultural proficiency. You must give them specific feedback on their performance with whole language, not just their ability to use isolated words and follow grammar formulas. Your students will know very quickly whether you've helped them learn to produce and comprehend language, and they will judge your value to them as a person who can or can't facilitate their growth in those areas. Students are in your room—and must by law and rule be in your room—to develop their ability in world language. If you don't or can't design learning situations that result in a proficiency product they can walk away and use, then your class is of little worth to students.

DESIGN FOR STUDENTS' INTERESTS, MOTIVATIONS, & STYLES

In addition to being drawn to the proficiency product that world language courses have to offer, the immediate topics and types of work can also be authentic to student preferences. Earlier we said that work must be personally meaningful to be engaging. Work may have personal meaning for a student because the content addresses a subject of interest, or because the task is designed to appeal to their learning preferences, or because it results in a product that is fulfilling to them or the people they care about.

While some students have a personal interest in world languages, not every student in our classrooms will. Some are there to fulfill college entrance requirements, some are there to fulfill graduation requirements, others wind up with us because there isn't room in their first elective choice. For those who take a genuine interest in your content, they would be happy to do any work you give them. For them, the content itself is the only necessary key to engagement. These students put in extra content hours regardless of the format of the activity, or who they get to work with, or whether or not there will be a grade.

For others who don't hold an intrinsic interest in the target language, you will need to design work for engagement based on the other topics that captivate them. For example, a video game is coming out next week and some students who struggle to connect with my content are excited about the game's debut. Knowing this, I plan a review game modeled on the format of the video game. Those students are excited to bring this game (normally a treat at home) into their classroom experience, so they happily spend the hour-long class actively engaged in reviewing the content. By addressing the interests of my students, I align with the third indicator of engagement, "The student's level of interest is sufficiently high that he persists in the face of difficulty." These students normally struggle to engage in content, but they persist because they love the game.

Further, by acknowledging their authentic personal interest in and skills with the game, I have grown in esteem in their eyes and built our working relationship so that the work they do for me also takes on a personal nature. Even a student who may be reluctant to engage in my content may become more engaged in units that tailor content to his interests. A unit on sports and fitness in the target language will be authentic to a student who is on the baseball and football teams because the subject already has personal meaning to him. Students may connect with the work on a personal level because of the content topic or because of the activity format.

Work may also touch on the motivators of a student. Part of what results in personal meaning is work which results in affirmation. A student may be motivated to create a product or learn a skill that the people they care about value. For example, a third-year language student volunteers to tutor an English learner. As the program progresses, the language student sees how her proficiency in the native language of the tutee is allowing the student to experience success at school, making the learner, his family, and the language student proud. While we design work that results in growth in proficiency, we must also be conscientious that the products of our work have real-world applications and that we provide opportunities for those products to be relevant and useful to the world. I can design an assessment to demonstrate proficiency in the classroom, or I can design an assessment that demonstrates proficiency because of its use in the world. For example, in an advanced ecology unit, I can assess students on their ability to talk about the literature, to present information in writing, or to comprehend audio programs. However, if I ask students to synthesize their work and create a PSA or flier in the target language and coordinate with a target language publication or broadcaster to get the winning entry aired in the community, then I have added a level of authenticity that will drive my students to develop their knowledge and work for the purpose of impacting their community for the better. Not only have I given my students the power of language, but I've also given them the power to be leaders in their community, to be participants on a global stage, and to accomplish a task that will have long-term meaning for themselves and those they serve.

Authenticity is about staying true to your students so that they can connect with your content in lasting and meaningful ways. Find tools, content, and products that your students are drawn to or driven by. The result will be higher levels of engagement and mastery, and the skills they learn will have permanence and durability because they are tied to an emotional experience like joy, pride, curiosity, or amusement. When you build that emotional connection between yourself, your students, and their work, everyone is empowered for learning.

BIG IDEAS

Authenticity is tied to the connections you have with your students. To achieve lasting and meaningful learning, teachers must know what authentic needs students have for using the language, and what authentic interests, motivators, and learning styles engage them. Schlechty's first indicator for engagement states, "The student sees the activity as personally meaningful." In other words, if we don't know what is personally meaningful to students, engagement will only be as deep as our relationship to and understanding of students. Because teaching and learning language are of primary importance to teachers, we often take for granted that world language content knowledge and proficiency may not be authentic goals of our learners. If we want our students to be able to connect with content, we must open doors to content through paths that are authentic to students. In other words, honoring and prioritizing their humanity takes precedence over pursuing proficiency. Similarly, it is the ways in which we connect with learners that allows them to build connections with content.

Questions for Reflection

1. Students often volunteer their connections to and experiences with language. What are some of the connections you have heard? How can you be intentional about building on that connection in the work you design for students?
2. What interests or motivations sometimes "distract" your students from engaging with content? What is one way you can flip that "distraction" into a tool for engagement in student work?
3. Who might be an authentic audience for your students? How can you design work for students that will reach that audience?
4. There will be times when basic challenges to the humanity of students take precedence over content. Give an example of a time when you "paused" content to meet your student's needs.

CHOICE

Students have some level of control over the work they do

CHOICE CONNECTS IN many ways with the other qualities of design, like authenticity or novelty and variety. Often the level of choices you can give will depend on the age of your students or the relationship of trust you have with them. The kinds of choices you offer will likely be validated by other major bodies of research like learning and personality styles, multiple intelligences, or differentiation. Simply put, choice is the level of autonomy students have in their environment, their grouping, their task, the content, or the product or result of their work.

As an adult, we often see choice in relation to the level of micromanaging imposed on us. Do we have to set the AC to a certain temperature? Do we have to meet weekly in content area teams? Do we have to submit lesson plans in the format of the District plan sheet? Many times, the choices we are allowed (or not allowed) to make reflect the amount of trust we perceive our superiors have in us, regardless of whether we understand why those choices have been made. The nature of school often dictates that the choices we can give regarding content are extremely limited (by District, State, or Federal standards and planning timelines). However, I would argue that in world language we have more liberty than most precisely because our standards relate to proficiency. If the standard is simply, "Student can present information on self, school, and home," then the student really has a lot of choice about his learning and what he'd like to share about himself in those areas. Many times, we limit students in world languages to the vocabulary list in the textbook, or the grammar point in the objectives, and we fail to see that, in doing so, we have taken away critical choices where students ask of themselves what knowledge would be important to them in those realms, or how they might go about telling others about themselves in real life, or what might be relevant to tell. All students have and are capable of asking those questions, but it is up to you as the expert in language study to create a place for asking them, to guide and direct the questions so that they lead to the discovery of content. In doing so, your content becomes authentically student-driven. I doubt that students will overlook the novelty of a teacher asking what they want to know and then providing time and resources for them to access it.

A good way to acknowledge student choice in content is with the Can-Do statements for your thematic units. Consider having students tailor their goals this way at the start of each unit:

Already Do:	Identify things you can already do to communicate about this topic. 1. 2. 3.
Need to Do:	Identify the things you still need to learn to do to communicate about this topic. 1. 2. 3. 4. 5.
Want to Do:	Identify things specific to your life that you would like to communicate about this topic. 1. 2. 3.

Can-Do Goals for World Language Classrooms

So many teachers are committed to top-down instruction, probably because there are so many layers of control over their design. There are national standards, state standards, district curriculum maps and pacing guides, and even department content area team updates. It's easy for a teacher to approach planning like a checklist, making sure her planning aligns with the expectations handed down to her from adults, rather than the needs and interests of her students. You can lead students to master your content without imposing it on them. In the chart above, the "Need to Do" section will be driven by standards but should be able to be arrived at by consensus and discussion.

Student experience and interests will be acknowledged in the "Already" and "Want" sections. Here's a student sample to demonstrate:

Topic:	Telling the News
Already Do:	1. *Get main ideas from news articles online* 2. *Tell what is happening* 3. *Talk about places*
Need to Do:	1. *Tell what happened* 2. *Use words related to news media (newspapers, reporters, video news)* 3. *Find details in news segments or articles* 4. *Use words about crime and accidents/disasters* 5. *Use big numbers and make currency conversions to understand amounts in the news*
Want to Do:	1. *Learn the exchange rate for mission trip* 2. *Do a news segment on morning announcements* 3. *Get better at irregular past tense*

Student Can-Do Sample

Aside from putting it on paper, how can a teacher acknowledge the skills a student already has (however rudimentary or advanced), and develop the skills a student seeks to master? If students are assessed on proficiency, then expecting them to demonstrate at least one of their "Already" skills and one skill they "Want" on the summative assessment, in addition to the required "Needs," would be a great way to honor their choice.

CHOICE IN ENVIRONMENT

While there are some areas that are difficult to allow student choice on, such as lighting or temperature, there are ways to incorporate environmental choice to at least recognize student desires. When your curriculum does open the door for environmental change, try to take advantage of it. By doing so, students have the chance to see the classroom differently (wherever and however it is that day), and hopefully, connect with student needs and interests at fundamental levels of "Where am I?" and "Do I like it here?" Here are some ways to change up the environment for a unit on giving directions. We would, of course, be executing these tasks using the target language:

- In small groups, hide your group's token in a secret location anywhere on campus. Write directions for another group to get from the classroom to your token. The group that finds your token will evaluate you on the quality of your directions.

- Students line up facing each other along a main hall. Give directions (turn right, step left, etc.) and see how well students can follow. There is instant feedback in this activity because students can look to their classmates for help, and there is protection because they have an opportunity to look and correct before they are judged. As they improve, raise the stakes by playing "Simon Says" style.

- If you have a ceiling drop-down style language lab, clear half the classroom, leaving only chairs and headsets. In the other half, line the desks up facing the headset side. As students answer, explain that the seated desks will be the "controllers," and the no-desk side will be the "robots." Give students a "cheat sheet" on a main board with essentials like "turn," "walk," or "until." Tell students to give their partner any directions they want, but the partner will only follow directions given in the target language. Halfway through the class, have students trade roles. My students LOVE this because they get to invent and direct. I can't count the times we've laughed together over the directions they come up with—a great team builder and trust-maker. I love it because they speak or listen to the target language for the duration of the class without my interference or coercion. If you really trust the group, offer to be their robot for the last few minutes of class after they've worn out and cleaned up.

On a day-to-day basis, you can give students control over some environmental options. For example, allow students to listen to the music of their choice while working. I find that even the option of having control over that little element of their work makes them more satisfied and attentive to it. Changing student seating is another way to refresh a student's environment. While there are some constraints to seating as you get to know students and their strengths (or weaknesses), you can often still give them choice. Here are some suggestions:

- Vary the seat groupings by number every few weeks so that you get different combinations of students working together (e.g., first two desks, then four, then three)
- Periodically select desks to swap. For example, when desks are in pairs, ask students at the door-side desk to find another seat. This new seat will be theirs until the next seating change.
- If your desks are normally grouped, try rows for a while and see how students do, or vice versa.

If I do have a student seating issue, I try to address it as students enter the room, rather than manage it publicly after students have already taken their seats. For example, if a struggling student is having trouble focusing next to a social high achiever, I'll simply ask him not to sit by his social partner for a while, or I may suggest that he sit by someone I know he works well with. You relieve peer pressure by directing the change, you honor the student's needs by getting him somewhere he can progress, and you give him the freedom to make choices that will benefit him.

Choice in Affiliation

1-day Restaurant Dialogue Scene	
Quickly form a group with a: -Smart device (Videographer) -Waiter -Restaurant Patron	Make a video of a scene in a restaurant in which you: • Order food • Comment on the food • Ask for something you need • Pay the bill. Post the video to the class blog.

An easier, and oft-used way to incorporate choice in a task is to allow student choice in grouping. Remember, an important component of collaboration is to accomplish a task that one person can't do alone. If you ask students to demonstrate their knowledge, some will prefer to work individually, some will gravitate toward a partner, some to a small group. If you consider the instances in which you may have been asked to work in a group, consider what purpose the group served. Did you have a role in the group? Could you have done the work without the presence of one or more group members? Did you benefit from the skills of individuals in your group? Your students are aware of those same issues and will look to you to set the expectations when it comes to affiliation or working interdependently. Each student has unique skills and abilities to offer, and teachers and students should consider them in the work that they do. Be conscientious of facilitating student work so that students have the chance to utilize their strengths to enhance their content mastery. Consider the following task:

Students have choice in their team. Students have choice in their role. Students have choice in the way they carry out the task. All students demonstrate proficiency in the task. Work is student-driven, and students must work efficiently with the target language to accomplish the task in the time provided. The teacher serves as an expert and guide and is able to attend to various groups as the need arises.

CHOICE IN TASK

We see many models about task choice with the rise of differentiation and multiple intelligences. You may have seen "Tic-tac-toe" tasks where students chose three tasks in a row from the board of choices, or vocabulary choice activities where students choose 20 points worth of vocab review activities from a list. These types of options give students choice based on learning style; however, they often lack authenticity. For example, no matter whether I make the 15-point vocabulary crossword with key, or the 15 picture vocab cards, I've benefited my recall, but not made a personally meaningful connection with the language. Another example of choice is a "Menu" where students choose one starter activity, one entree (big idea activity), and one side dish or dessert (maybe an alternate learning style or "fun" media choice). You can tailor each section of the menu to address content standards, modes, learning styles, difficulty level, etc. A great example from the blog of Megan Johnston and Kara Parker, "The Creative Language Class," is their Real World

Homework[11]. They designed a stampable "Real World" handout that features everyday tasks that connect students with the target language, on which students earn credit through contact with the language. Some examples might be to try a new target culture recipe, listen to a target language song, or to find the target language in advertising or at the grocery store. This activity is awesome because it makes students the real workers of knowledge. They seek out and experiment with language firsthand. They get feedback and affirmation from the teacher. My favorite part of this activity is that the work they do involves the world around them and asks them to connect with language in the ways they naturally find it. Their work will be unique and personally driven.

In an activity like "Real World Homework," students have choice in which task to complete, they make decisions about how to complete the task, and they are responsible for choosing which resources to use. To an extent, risk is also embedded in these activities (ordering food in the target language vs. printing a target language recipe) and students concerned with risk get to choose an activity they are comfortable with.

Choice in Content

Some of you are already asking how we can give students choice in content when we have standards to follow. Let's continue to use the example of "Real World Homework" from the last section. In the blog sample, students were developing proficiency communicating with others according to a predetermined (probably ACTFL) level regarding eating and food in the target language. Each student would encounter thematic language in different ways authentic to the experience they have. There will be different ingredients in every recipe. Servers in restaurants may have different ways of speaking. Songs will have different choruses. However, despite the diversity of language they encounter through these tools, they will all have the end result of being better prepared to use the target language when it comes to eating and food. The outcome, or product, is language proficiency. Rather than ensure that students can use a formula or identify the significance of an event, world

---

11   Parker, K. (2012, February 14). Real World Homework. Retrieved September 18, 2016, from http://www.creativelanguageclass.com/real-world-homework/

language objectives require that students communicate according to a standard of proficiency appropriate to their course level or progress.

Of course, proficiency is guided by the "must know" of vocabulary and structure, but fluency is where students can flourish in the shades of meaning, innuendo, colloquialisms, mannerisms, and regional traditions. Those elements are as much a part of successful communication as noun-adjective agreement and verb conjugations. Allow your students an opportunity to delve into content in a way that stresses proficiency over perfection, so that they can begin to feel their way through language as much as they can read or write it. Instead of deciding for yourself what content is valuable and relevant, design learning opportunities that empower your students with the autonomy to seek out and use content in ways that are authentic to their needs and interests. Allowing for student choice in content is satisfying in and of itself, but by acknowledging student choice in content, students are responsible for discovering ways that world language is already present and meaningful in their own lives.

CHOICE IN PRODUCT

At the most superficial level, we give students choices to create products that demonstrate proficiency. In the restaurant skit earlier, the end product (a video dialogue) would be the result of many choices in language, food preference, and technology. What we didn't ask, though, is, "What effect will this activity have on the world as a result?" For the student, the answer is simply that she is able to order food in the target language. At a deeper level though, it's important to remind ourselves of the more noble purposes of language. Consider ways in which your products can connect with students on the level of personal meaning and purpose. The third indicator of engagement is "the student finds the task sufficiently challenging that she believes she will accomplish something of worth by doing it." Have you given your students the choice of taking on a challenge that will accomplish something of worth? As a language teacher, of course I believe that language (the content) holds inherent worth for any learner, but not all of my students feel that way. Giving them choice about the products of their learning is a way to teach what must be taught, but respect individual needs and interests.

BIG IDEAS

When we talk about the design qualities for engagement, if we say a student responds to choice, we mean they are more engaged when they have more autonomy in their work. Choice in world language work can take many forms, such as choice in:

- Environment
- Affiliation
- Task
- Content
- Product

While superficial choices such as seating arrangement or task type are easy to modify, teachers should consider at what level students have choices in the curriculum. Are standards mandated from afar and presented with top-down instruction, or do they emerge more organically through student-driven learning?

Questions for Reflection

1. What do you appreciate having control of in your own work environment? What do you wish you could control?
2. What choices do you allow your students to make during a typical day? What do they get to decide or control?
3. What do students have control over in their learning? Do those choices have a tangible impact on how students master content?
4. What choices do students get to make in their assessment?

PRODUCT FOCUS

Work results in a product or performance

THE PRIMARY PRODUCT of a world language class is proficiency. The work that you design for students must result in their ability to perform with language. Learning a foreign language is entirely about performance because without using language proficiently, communication cannot happen. The "language" of intercultural competence is interwoven into this performance as well, inasmuch as following cultural norms, expectations, and traditions are part of understanding and being understood in another country. As you teach each unit, the proficiency of that performance is exactly where your students need feedback so that they can continue to grow in ability. If the product of your unit is, "Student can use and recognize forty terms and three grammar points," then you haven't assessed proficiency. That is not to say that their proficiency doesn't include the terms and grammar, but that students can know words and rules for grammar and not have proficiency. The work that world language teachers design for students must be work that results in the ability to communicate. That communication is the product students will be able to perform. Later when we focus on assessment, we'll look at some proficiency performance rubrics to help give students the feedback they need to get performance results they can use.

WHEN STUDENTS NEED MORE

For those students who are not inherently motivated to communicate in a second language, other products of learning are also valuable. For example, if you tie students' work to a real-world result like being published in a local paper, or having their work used on the system website for parents who speak the target language, then one of the results of their work is having an opportunity to be published. In addition to performance, you've linked student work to another design quality that appeals to them: affirmation from the community. I would say that the more design qualities you incorporate in student work, the more likely its success with your students, but that's not necessarily how it will work. You must know what drives your students in order to know what design qualities will result in their mastery of the content. Let me give you an example of my own:

> Personally, I'm very driven by novelty and variety. I get excited about language and I like to do lots of fun and exciting things with it. I found, though, that some of my student groups started complaining when I planned what I thought were fun interpersonal speaking activities or great games like Black Ops Review (designed based on a video game). My students said things like, "Can't we just have a study guide?" "I don't want to move all over the place." "Do we have to talk to people again?" What they were really saying is that they wanted to work quietly and individually at their desk with some clearly organized content. Where I had been excited about novelty and affiliation, they were concerned with organization of knowledge and clear and compelling product standards. It's not that my activities weren't good ideas, they just weren't good activities for those groups. To get those groups of students successfully to the performance levels I anticipated, I had to design work in line with the qualities that they valued. Their values were different from mine, but we had a common performance goal.

DISCRETE SKILL OR PROFICIENCY PRODUCT?

I would encourage you to consider also what proficiency product the work has for a student. It's easy to design work to address a specific grammar point or vocabulary list, and those skills do contribute to proficiency, but they may not have an overt proficiency product. If your unit is broken into work that addresses specific daily topics, but you seek a proficiency product at the end of the unit, your students will have difficulty linking the daily tasks with developing fluency. If you expect a proficiency-based assessment at the conclusion of a unit, your work throughout the unit should be proficiency-based.

To help illustrate this point, I've drafted two lesson plan models to meet a single objective. While they both contain valuable and viable learning tasks, they are not both proficiency-oriented. As you read through the models on the following page, consider what choices and tasks you might use in your own classroom.

"Describing Myself" Unit Objectives:

I can describe my appearance and the appearance of others.

I can ask about the appearance of others.

	Model 1	Model 2
Day 1	Teacher (T) models appearance vocabulary in target language (TL) presentation. Students (Ss) complete vocab puzzles.	Ss work with T to come up with a class "must have" vocabulary list that fulfills the objectives. Ss groups sign up to investigate a vocab topic like "girl clothing" or "describing hair" and work starts.
Day 2	T reviews vocab slideshow with Ss and collects puzzles. T follows up with powerpoint with sample photos of people. Ss volunteer to identify appearance adjectives evident in photos. Ss complete handout identifying adjectives that describe people.	Ss share "must have" vocab work in a shared google document available to the class. T models work by sketching a quick picture of self and labeling with relevant adjectives from each section of vocab list generated by Ss. Ss create own self-portraits, labeling with vocab from Ss-generated list.
Day 3	T (re)introduces the TL verb "to be." Ss take notes. After some modeling by the teacher, Ss complete a cloze activity filling in the correct form of the verb for the sentence. In the next section of the work, students write 5 simple sentences using the verb and adjectives to describe people they know.	T models how to talk about others by using Ss work samples "Paula is tall. Paula has brown eyes." T asks Ss to trade portraits and get into small groups. Without disclosing identity of portrait, Ss describe classmate pictured until team members correctly identify him/her. T asks Ss to write three sentences describing each person pictured in their group's work.
Day 4	T models the question "How is/What's he like?" to find out what someone looks like. T asks students questions, referring to students in the room. Ss do pair activity in which they ask each other about the appearance of celebrities.	_Interpersonal Speaking Situation_: _Since you drive, you volunteered to pick up the siblings of three friends from camp today, but you realize you don't know which children are the siblings. Call your friends and get a description to find them._ T models how to ask what someone looks like. Ss silently select three classmates who they will describe as their "siblings." Partners ask for a description and guess which classmates are their "siblings" based on description.
Day 5 Assess- ment	Quiz: Part 1.) Listen to the description and write the number under the picture/person described. Part 2.) Fill in the blanks with the forms of "to be" Part 3.) Answer the question by writing what the people look like. (Ex. What does Principal Martin look like? He is tall and has brown eyes.).	Interpersonal Speaking Assessment: A tornado just passed. They're evacuating the school to make sure everyone is ok and get them to their families. Your friend calls and you agree to help each other find your moms. Ask and answer your friend's questions according to the guide that follows. As your friend describes his mom, make a quick sketch that represents her appearance. You will have time following the dialogue to finish the sketch, and you may make note of keywords in the space provided to guide your sketch. Script Guide: -_Thanks for helping, friend._ Respond to your friend (You're welcome.)- -_Your friend asks a question (What's your mom look like?)._ Respond to your friend- -_Ok, I'll look._ Ask what your friend's mom looks like.- -_Friend describes mom. Well, talk to you soon._

Both units address the same objectives over the same time period, likely from a beginning first-year unit. Here's how they compare:

1. If we work from the premise that students are the knowledge workers who are to discover and build their knowledge, and the teacher's role is as an expert consultant who gives feedback and provides direction, then Model 2 portrays those roles. Model 2 also shows a high level of affiliation because students work interdependently in order to complete tasks and develop proficiency. In model 1, work is organized, presented, and provided by the teacher. The teacher does a lot of performing, while the students "absorb" knowledge. There is minimal novelty or variety because the format of the lessons is predictable from day to day. There is a high level of structure and organization, but very little choice or authenticity because everything is teacher-driven.

2. Model 1 focuses primarily on written proficiency, rarely practices speaking, and does not formally assess speaking proficiency at all. Model 2 builds a foundation of speaking proficiency from which writing, listening, and reading are the resultant products. If we are using a proficiency-based model with a foundation in the ACTFL Proficiency Guidelines, and assume that these are first semester, first-year learners who have a Novice Mid proficiency target, then we know that:

> Writers at the Novice Mid sublevel can reproduce from memory a modest number of words and phrases in context. They can supply limited information on simple forms and documents… Novice Mid writers exhibit a high degree of accuracy when writing on well-practiced, familiar topics using limited formulaic language… Errors in spelling or in the representation of symbols may be frequent. There is little evidence of functional writing skills. (ACTFL Proficiency Guidelines, 2012)

> To assess a learner who probably has minimal functional writing skills seems like a great risk for the learner and teacher. If we assume

that the teacher has done a fantastic job of drilling the vocabulary list, then all students will respond with the same limited formulaic language, negating any influence of choice or authenticity in their product.

As speakers, however, their proficiency target reads, "Speakers at the Novice Mid sublevel communicate minimally by using a number of isolated words and memorized phrases limited by the particular context in which the language has been learned." (ACTFL Proficiency Guidelines 2012) Model 2 seeks minimal, memorized phrases for communicating meaning, it allows for authenticity by allowing students to describe people authentic to their lives in authentic ways, and it holds students responsible for comprehension. The assessment is a natural product similar in format to the work students have done over the course of the unit.

3. Some of you will argue that either model can result in proficiency. Parts of both models can result in proficiency depending on your students. Taken as an entire unit, Model 1 lacks novelty and variety, has no opportunity for students to make their own choices, does not incorporate any authentic connection between students and proficiency, and never allows students to work as a team. The lessons show high levels of organization and clear standards, but is it compelling to fill in blanks with verb forms? Is describing a textbook picture a situation that relates to real life? I find, for the sake of classroom management (and personal sanity), by building authenticity, choice, affiliation, and novelty into the work I design, along with a healthy dose of content, organization, and clear standards, that Model 2 tends to lend itself to the safe, team- & proficiency-driven classroom my students and I seek. An environment heavy in team-driven success helps develop a low level of risk and opens doors for students to understand and own their proficiency level.

Worthy Products

Many times in teaching, our focus is so intense on making sure students know how our content can benefit them, that we forget to address the question of how it can benefit others. Bigger than what learning a language can do for an individual student is the power of words and literacy in the world. We do a disservice to our students if we show them the words, but don't give them the opportunity to use the power of words for the good of others. As you design work and assessments that are proficiency focused, also consider these elements of the product you envision for them:

- Does the product of their work have immediate use in the community?
- Is there a community or world need for the results of your students' work?
- Can the result of a student's work be used to help anyone beyond the student himself?
- Will the student consider that this product is "something of worth?" Engagement Standard 3 reads "the student finds the task sufficiently challenging that she believes she will accomplish something of worth by doing it."[12]

If we ask these questions of our work and of our students, the result will be students who have a worldview that includes service to others. By revealing that something that benefits them is also something that can benefit the world, much more is at stake in their learning. Think of the impact it would have on learning if the student knows that the product they are responsible for can benefit people they care about in meaningful ways. Is that something of worth? Will success matter more or less? Will their persistence and motivation drive them to overcome obstacles or will it be easy to "take a grade" and move on?

---

12   *Schlechty Center On Engagement.* 1st ed. Schlechty Center, 2015. Web. 12 May 2015.

BIG IDEAS

As teachers, we see the primary product that we offer students is progress towards proficiency in world language. As believers in design, we know that the important quality of an engaging product is that students value it. If we are offering communicative proficiency, is that truly a product students value?

Questions for Reflection

1. For students engaged by a proficiency product, what do you do to support them?
2. For students not engaged by communicative proficiency, what else does your class offer?
3. Does the work your students do impact your community?
4. Share an example of a time when you helped a student realize the power of their words.

Clear and Compelling
Standards + Assessment

Knowing exactly what is expected of you and
being compelled to demonstrate mastery

AT ITS FOUNDATION, the learning of our students revolves around the standards they are expected to master. The nature of studying world language, or any other subject, is that important parts of content mastery are constantly evolving given our current context in the world, along with the advances, changes, or discoveries being made by those we consider "experts." Slang for social networks, recognition of indigenous histories, or even "official" changes to target language alphabets or dictionaries are just a few examples of ways daily life meets learning in world language. Whether or not students keep up with and master content ultimately depends on whether or not they feel compelled to do so. Many things may compel them—parents, pop culture, intrinsic interest, getting into college, working with a partner—and we will group those factors into the categories of the ten design qualities we have built this book around. If, in language, the primary objectives are proficiency of use and knowledge of socio-cultural context, then we must communicate a very clear definition of what "proficiency" means and what it looks like at different levels.

As students develop proficiency, assessment (by self, peer, or teacher) is the tool that will communicate what success looks like and what progress students need to make to reach the next level of proficiency. It is important to note also that the qualities that make a student want to do work will be the same qualities that will compel a student toward an assessment because the assessment will give them feedback on their progress towards mastering the work. Just as students seek value in work, students will seek value in the tools their teachers use to give them feedback. If your tool for assessment is not considered valid, or the feedback is not helpful, then students may not be compelled to demonstrate their mastery of content.

Since world language standards are proficiency-based, it is equally important that assessments be proficiency-based. Some teachers use rubrics that include criteria like:

- Did the student use each form of the past tense?
- How many vocabulary words were included?
- How many structural errors are present?
- Is the brochure neat and does it include color?

If these kinds of criteria drive your assessment, then it fails to give students feedback on fluency in a way that allows them to advance. You may consider these things to be important details, but they should not drive the feedback you give. First and foremost, students need to know if they are effective communicators.

Think of your own experience as a language learner. Before you achieved fluency, you were able to communicate, even though you may have struggled to find the right word or use the correct ending. To help, you may have resorted to pointing or gesturing. You were probably able to understand much more than you were able to say, so you could follow or participate in a conversation, even though you weren't as competent in language as your native-speaking partner. These are important steps toward fluency in language that you should recognize in your students. Is getting language correct important? Yes! The richness and accuracy with which students speak or write are what will distinguish them as Novice, Intermediate, or Advanced with language; however, forcing correct production at the expense of communication or comprehension can diminish proficiency.

So how do we go about developing a proficiency rubric for everyday use that students can use with as much ease as teachers? ACTFL's Proficiency Guidelines are a wonderful tool, as are your district's curriculum, but those tools are teacher tools and are not designed for day-to-day use as feedback for content mastery. Below are some basic guidelines that I would encourage you to consider as you design your assessment.

Guidelines for Designing Assessment

1. **Use the Language of the ACTFL Proficiency Guidelines**

   Does your assessment tool give feedback using language from ACTFL's Proficiency Guidelines? Help your students learn to articulate where they are (Novice High, Intermediate Low). Doing so gives your assessments consistency which makes your expectations clear every time, for the duration of the course. Also, by using a "sliding scale" of achievement, your students can see that proficiency is about more than getting an A on a test. They can set goals and target areas of weakness to drive their proficiency to the next level. Further, students begin to understand that communication is more important than checking boxes on a rubric. When assessment is framed from a communication standpoint, students begin to learn how multi-faceted communication is. They begin to understand how the way they speak is as important as the words they speak. They realize that the comprehension of their listener is as important as their ability to say the words. As a shortcut when I model for my students, I often nickname proficiency targets based on year of study. For example, in response to "What are you wearing," I could expect a first-year student to say, "I wear a red shirt and pants." A second-year answer might be, "I'm wearing a striped, red shirt with buttons, jean shorts, and sandals. A third-year answer might be, "I'm wearing a striped, red shirt made of cotton that I bought at H&M, with jean shorts and comfortable leather sandals." By providing a continuum of proficiency that models a variety of language and structure, students can see that the depth and variety of language they manipulate are what primarily defines their proficiency. They reframe their objective from completion of a task to development of a skill.

2. **Use the assessment tool without giving a grade**

Yes, I know you need to give grades, but not at first, and not always. Give students feedback with the tool so they know you are investing in their success, not calculating their average. Ask the students to assess themselves and have an honest discussion about what they find out. Ask students to assess each other because they will learn more about what their success looks like when they see it in someone else first. Each time a student attempts the task and reflects on their performance, they are able to identify how they would improve it and solidify how they can maintain it. By using the same type of assessment for formative and summative evaluation, students build a picture of proficiency with goals they can attain.

3. **Keep it simple**

Assessment is a tool for *students*, and it should be designed for them. Organize it in a way that is easy to follow and use language that your students understand. Some of your students, special needs in particular, will have a hard time discerning the subtleties of one proficiency level to the next, so keep the target concisely worded, but broad in concept. For example, a Novice Low response manages key words and memorized phrases. Novice High can communicate with simple sentences with few errors that interrupt.

4. **Set levels for grading from the same tool that you use to set levels of proficiency**

ACTFL targets should impact your rubric's expectations because they lay out how a learner is expected to perform at a given proficiency level. ACTFL performance targets show that a first-semester student is likely to have Novice-Low to-Mid writing performance, and second-semester students should demonstrate Novice-High performance. What kind of performance earns full marks will be different from first semester to second because we expect to see developing proficiency. Communicative proficiency has a snowball effect. Proficiency grows over time, adding more pieces than it loses, but with a constantly changing outward appearance. Teachers should expect students to use vocabulary with variety and depth, but they should also expect mastering the structure and nuance of language to evolve with repetition and practice. Through the rubric, the teacher creates a path and a plan by which students can reflect on their own evolution and set goals for incorporating new skills. Without a rubric that seeks growth over skills, then student focus will remain on the skill of the moment, and cumulative growth will carry less importance than momentary mastery. Grades, then, are separate from, but intertwined with proficiency, and should mark milestones of achievement much like a portfolio might demonstrate the different accomplishments and skills of an artist or architect.

5. **Include at least one "next-step"**

Include at least one "next-step" for those students who are ready to move beyond expectations, or to recognize the abilities of heritage or native speakers. Particularly in the case of heritage speakers, many will appreciate having a common language to talk about their proficiency with their non-native peers. While these students will likely perform very well in comprehension tasks, their skills at production, knowledge of cultural context for countries other than their own, or ability to sustain conversation are skills at which they can compete with peers.

There are a lot of great proficiency-based learning tools available (for free). Some of my favorites were the Performance Assessment Rubric designed by the World Languages Cohort of Jefferson County Public Schools (JCPS) in Kentucky under the leadership of Thomas Sauer and Greg Duncan in 2011. They developed great materials that include a comprehensive proficiency rubric, self-reflection checklists, and sample units with assessments. Their rubric is comprehensive for any student in modern language levels 1-3 and includes a place for Minor Focus details that a teacher may wish to highlight in a task. The rubric does not show a grade, but the system has aligned target proficiency levels with Performance Grading Guidelines according to year and semester of the learner. Kara Parker and Megan Smith of CreativeLanguageClass.com created a similar Proficiency Rubric inspired by their work with JCPS and

Duncan. Several years later in 2015, JCPS released their World Languages Curricula to the public. The revisions include Performance Assessments with each unit, and performance rubrics by age (primary/secondary student), and by performance mode. All documents are available to the public online at no cost. Sara-Elizabeth Cottrell of the blog Musicuentos has several posts related to the JCPS resources, along with her own redesigned Performance to Proficiency World Language Assessment Rubric to address some of the concerns she had for her and her colleagues' classroom. The Foreign Language Educators of New Jersey (FLENJ) also teamed up with Greg Duncan and the Foreign Language Assistance Program (FLAP) in the Consortium for Assessing Performance Standards (CAPS) to come up with proficiency rubrics. They have cumulative speaking and writing rubrics similar to the one by JCPS, as well as rubrics broken down by proficiency level, purpose (presentational, interpersonal, interpretive), and mode (reading, writing, speaking, listening). Since this rubric is targeted to a novice-mid proficiency on an interpersonal task, the students will know from the ratings if they have met or exceeded the performance expectation. There are few criteria and clearly written expectations so that feedback can happen quickly and be easily understood by students. The Center for Advanced Language Acquisition (CARLA) of the University of Minnesota also has an impressive array of resources for language teachers. They offer an entire site with modules, tutorials, and templates for Content-Based Second Language Instruction. The Center for Applied Linguistics offers the Foreign Language Assessment Directory, "a free, searchable directory of information on more than 200 tests in over 90 languages." If you're interested and able to spend a little money, ACTFL's *Implementing Integrated Performance Assessments* and *Keys to Assessing Language Performance* books are available for purchase online.

Design qualities will compel a student toward learning. Standards will define to what learning the teacher guides students. Assessment will be the feedback that tells students how far their learning has taken them. Student product will be the benefits they gain from proficiency.

To achieve that proficiency product, students must know what steps, or standards, to master. Let's take the example of a multi-story building.

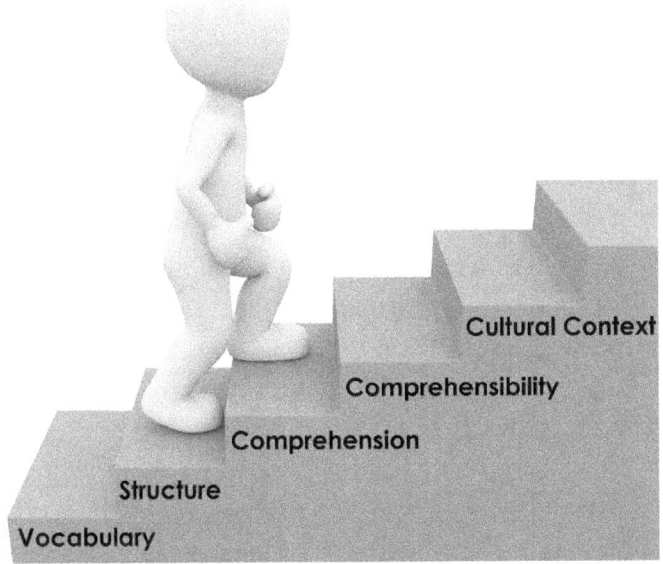

Steps to Proficiency

The proficiency levels are represented by the floors, or levels, of the building. The stairs would be the criteria that define that proficiency level, and the steps themselves would be built of "can do" statements particular to the thematic unit being covered. To reach the top, or fluency, students must master "can do" formative tasks such as "Student can interpret information about taking the train to a destination." Their proficiency at carrying out the task will bring them closer to advancing to the next level. For example, to make the next step from Novice-Mid to Novice-High, a student who hears the information once or twice and comprehends is ready to advance, whereas a student who needs to hear the information repeatedly and more slowly is not ready to advance in proficiency.

The teacher is the designer that will guide students to the tools they need to advance from step to step, and level to level. To design in a way that will lead up to ever-increasing proficiency, the teacher must design with a thorough understanding of how the path to the proficiency looks, and with an equally intense understanding of what challenges she will face as she guides students through engagement to mastery.

Big Ideas

If the definition of world language proficiency is what sets the standards for learning, then assessment is how we measure progress towards proficiency. Good assessment tools clearly and consistently align with our definition of proficiency, are written for students to understand, and provide opportunities for low-risk feedback, as well as recognition of growing "beyond" expectations. The design qualities we incorporate into our proficiency tasks are what makes them compelling. Our assessments should provide feedback on what next steps are needed to "level up" with language.

Questions for Reflection

Think of an upcoming unit of study as you answer the following questions:

1. What are the anticipated performance levels for student comprehension and production? What descriptors does ACTFL use to describe targeted proficiency at their level across presentational, interpretive, and interpersonal tasks?
2. What cultural competencies do you want students to develop rooted in the context of the unit? How will you assess their progress?
3. What opportunities will students have to receive proficiency feedback before receiving a grade?
4. How will your students know what to do to improve before the end-of-unit assessment?

CONTENT AND SUBSTANCE

High-quality intellectual work, rich and profound knowledge

AS WORLD LANGUAGE teachers, proficiency is our desired result, or product, for our students. Standards are statements of what we expect students to do with language and will determine evidence of proficiency. Content and substance are the resources, materials, and curricula we use for learning. Our description of "Content and Substance" indicates that these materials should result in high-quality intellectual work and rich and profound knowledge. For our purposes, we will consider "profound" to imply knowledge that is penetrating, insightful, meaningful, and even transformative.

Before we go too far into exploring content, I need to stress two points. First, "Content and Substance" is a design quality, or characteristic of work, that may or may not factor into a student's engagement. There are students who just aren't interested in doing profound intellectual work with your content. That's where the other design qualities come into play as you design work with qualities that will engage your students. Second, as a teacher, some of your content is non-negotiable. It must be addressed for students to achieve proficiency. Therefore, how you approach content and which substance, or materials, you choose are elements within your control. Addressing those elements will be the key to making your content engaging for students who don't have an intrinsic interest in the content.

With this in mind, this chapter has four goals. First, we will examine ways to build depth into the content. Next, we will consider how to select substance (materials) of quality. Then, we will develop strategies for incorporating other design qualities when interest in content isn't enough. Lastly, we will discuss the role of our content in connecting our learners to their own voice and vision, and to one another.

BUILDING RICH & PROFOUND CONTENT KNOWLEDGE

I will assume that your units develop student proficiency in a way that revolves around a contextual theme. To this end, you will likely organize some basic vocabulary and grammatical skills that will be fundamental for that unit. However, your unit will not grow out of these skills, rather they will be a byproduct as students develop their competence communicating about the theme. Students may master skills, but their ability to communicate will not develop unless your unit, and their assessment, is driven by proficiency goals. As students delve into language in a deep and meaningful way, the knowledge that they acquire will allow them to advance in proficiency. High-quality work will be the key to getting students engaged in content in a meaningful way that leads to mastery.

Let's explore this topic from the vantage of a sample novice unit and break down some ways to build depth of content. We'll call our sample unit "What I like to do." In accordance with the unit's title, we'll assume that the necessary skills are discussing activities students like and using structures for expressing likes. While the ability to talk about these common activities would be "must know" knowledge for basic proficiency, things which are common will not be very rich. If your students are aware that advancing in proficiency is a reflection of the richness and depth with which one can communicate, and their success (grade) is a reflection of proficiency as well, students will begin to take advantage of the "extras" to give their own language use a sense of richness as well.

For the sake of organization, having a list of "must knows" is a good place to start, but we must also be careful not to limit students by dictating which words are "the right" words. If we do, we have essentially "de-skilled" them. "De-skilling" is to take away skills and opportunities for learning from a student. When we say, "Here's the vocab list and grammar notes. They're what you need to know for the test," we have taken away the learner's opportunity to discover and develop language for himself. He does not have to do much intellectual work at all, and class work will result in the same basic language tools for every learner, denying any student the chance to connect with language in a profound and personal way. Likewise, your assessment may "de-skill" a language learner. If all your tests have a vocabulary matching section, a listening multiple-choice section, and a reading short answer section, then all your tests assess student ability at a fixed and unchanging depth of knowledge. Except for minor variations in content, students will never be asked to demonstrate, nor receive feedback on, their proficiency beyond that level. Many students are driven by organization and structure and need the vocabulary list as a starting place for learning, but neither should it be the ending place of learning. Instead, we might say, "Here are some fundamental words for talking about common likes. For our end-of-unit assessments, you will need to be able to discuss what you and your friends like to do in your free time. Remember your proficiency rubric as you organize the words you will need to do so."

To add depth, build proficiency, and appeal to choice and authenticity, it is important to ask your students to connect learning with their own experiences and the lives of others. Our sample unit, "What I like to do," opens the door to communication that reaches into many thematic realms. The College Board recommends six themes for AP Spanish Language[13]:

1. Families and Communities
2. Science and Technology
3. Beauty and Aesthetics
4. Contemporary Life
5. Global Challenges
6. Personal and Public Identities

Even at the novice level, it is easy to see how student learning will touch on many of these themes. Talking about one's likes will easily incorporate language relating to family, technology, and contemporary life. As they begin to talk about their own interests, framing them in these realms allows students to make comparisons between their own leisure activities, those of their peers, and to begin to connect with preferences of speakers in the countries of study. The way their lives connect with others, with their community, and with the world transforms the content from simple to profound. Talking about after-school activities becomes a conversation about topics like school life, eating schedules, poverty and wealth, and family traditions. This depth

13   College Board AP Central. (2019). AP Spanish language and culture: Course and exam description. Retrieved from https://apcentral.collegeboard.org/pdf/ap-spanish-language-and-culture-course-and-exam-description-1.pdf?course=ap-spanish-language-and-culture

provides authenticity to content in which students invest in themselves to understand their role in the world of others. Communicating in the target language becomes the vehicle that drives that deeper understanding.

Tapping into individual student interests and allowing students to cultivate a unique personal vocabulary for talking about themselves and their friends would be one way to add richness to their language knowledge. Let's say for our unit, that one of your students likes to bake. Other students may not like to cook because they must prepare meals for siblings while parents work. Others might like to eat in restaurants. All of these experiences contribute to a connected conversation among learners about their likes. If we push our conversation outside the boundaries of national borders, it might be relevant to discuss that few homes in the Caribbean have or use ovens. In the conversation about why, students will draw on knowledge about climate, economics, and history. Granted, the level at which these discussions can happen will vary depending on year of study but using language at any level to develop this understanding is high-quality intellectual work!

SELECTING QUALITY MATERIALS

The materials we ask students to use for work should be rich in language and reflect the perspectives of the societies that produced them. This depth of context will naturally generate student questions out of necessity (What is that word?) and out of curiosity (Why do they do it that way?). The way we use materials may be bound by time and the proficiency of our students, but the sources themselves need not be forced to fit those same constraints. There are four qualities to look for in a resource that will lead to high-quality intellectual work.

Materials Connect with Prior Learning & Provide Clues for New Learning

We know that the more our work connects with students' prior knowledge, the more easily it will be interpreted and integrated into their learning. As we study modern languages, this scaffolding may connect with students' experiential knowledge on topics like personal hygiene or sports, or with language material they have previously studied, such as identifying or describing people using subject pronouns and adjectives. Let's say we've chosen a magazine spread, commercial, or music video in the target language about likes.

Experiential knowledge will connect us to the many of the activities shown and probably to the format of the media if it is a product, artist, or magazine we're familiar with. Images in the material will allow students to infer meaning as they work. The format of the material may also give clues that students can use to infer or identify important information. For example, bolded or italicized words in articles, labels on graphs, titles of works of art or literature can draw students' attention to language "keys" that will allow them to unlock the meaning of text or social context in a work. Students can draw on their knowledge of English to infer the meaning of cognates. Also, the fact that our material deals with the unit of study—in this case, peoples' likes—means that it will hit on some of the common language from our unit's "must know" list. All of those connections will open the door to allowing students to dive confidently into unfamiliar language and context. It is the unfamiliar situation-specific vocabulary, structures, and cultural contexts that will result in deep, high-level learning.

Material is Designed for an Authentic Target Audience

The target, in this case, is speakers of the target language. Those materials which will result in high-level, intellectual, rich, and profound work will be those that have as an audience speakers of the target language. Further, if students are working toward proficiency with materials that are also authentic for them, then materials that exist in the world outside of their classroom will be more true to their lives than those created by a teacher for classroom use. In some specific situations, it's not always easy to find authentic materials to represent a particular point, and sometimes the best practice for a student's need is practice tailored by a teacher. In this instance, the teacher is meeting the authentic need of bridging the gap between a student's comprehension and the content so that the student can move forward. However, be careful that this is not standard practice. Students who are driven by the quality of the content they are studying will not be satisfied with classroom materials invented primarily by the teacher or textbook author because they are not materials designed for a native audience. Further, without using authentic resources, the course will fail to align with many of the recommendations of ACTFL, the College Board AP program, IB programs, or be sufficient preparation for college, work, or travel.

Material Represents a Relevant Time Period for the Unit of Study

Those topics which focus on contemporary life should be represented with contemporary materials. Conceptual or thematic units, particularly in more advanced levels of study should incorporate important historic material of reference. Here I use the word "historic" to mean that it has significance in the world in a given location and place in time, whether it be the last 5 years, 50 years, or 500 years. Historic works of art, notable literature, advances in mathematics or science, and political speeches are all examples of materials that help learning a language become multi-dimensional. Suddenly language has a place in history, geography, and technological development. These connections contribute to activating the prior knowledge we talked about earlier, and in building new, lasting, profound knowledge for our learners.

Material Connects with Student Interests, Experiences, and Goals

In the chapter titled <u>Authenticity</u>, we determined that authentic work satisfies the authentic purposes, needs, and desires of the student. Therefore, the materials that we choose will be the tool we use to satisfy our students. A strong relationship with your students will inform your search for materials because you know who will be most likely to engage with a particular source. Are there students who play sports or instruments? Do any have jobs? Do their families come from other countries? What kind of homes do they live in? Have they ever been to the beach or to a play? Consider the potential limits of your students' experiences and background knowledge. Consider how their dreams and goals connect with your content. Textbook authors don't know your students. They will provide you with resources, but not necessarily the ones your students need to go into the world, talk about themselves, and find out about others. Using resources that don't recognize the experiences and goals of your students puts you at risk of closing doors on engagement for them. The realia you choose gives you the opportunity to find material about people your students identify with, despite being thousands of miles away, speaking another language, and living immersed in a different history. Take advantage of realia to empower your students to see the same-ness between themselves and people of the world.

CONNECTING WHEN CONTENT ISN'T ENOUGH

If you're like me, you got into the business of teaching world languages because they were an important part of your life, and you felt confident that you could help others who wanted to make your language an important part of their lives too. Many early and middle grades teachers have the benefit of being a novelty for young students. Their class is one of few with a different teacher, new kinds of activities, and perhaps a room change. However, at the high school novice level, many students wind up in world language classrooms to fulfill college requirements or at their parents' insistence, maybe even because they thought foreign language was the least threatening elective. Students often don't start learning a language convinced that our content really holds meaning for them. Your passion and the way you connect their lives to the world through language will be what draws them towards content.

In the meantime, as you design work for students, be sure to design in ways that appeal to the design qualities that are important for your students. If they find the work engaging only because they get to work with a partner or watch a music video, that's okay because they are still doing the work! As you take the time to design work that is personally meaningful to students and results in a product they value, students will take the time to persist in the face of difficulty until they can succeed with the content.

CONNECTING CONTENT TO OPPORTUNITY

Selecting content and materials to meet your students' needs and interests has an impact in our community far beyond the impact it will have tomorrow on your students' engagement. In addition to engagement and interest, we also have to begin talking the language of success. We do this daily by minimizing risk in the classroom, but how is the language you use and teach your students preparing them for success beyond your classroom? So you've made your students aware of other cultures, but have you also prepared them to gracefully be the "other" when the time comes? One opportunity we have in the language classroom, even more than any other content, is a discussion of "otherness." What unites us? What makes us different? How do we respond sensitively to differences? How is otherness important?

Paul Tough offers some thoughts on otherness and belonging in his article, "Who Gets to Graduate?" from the NY Times (2014). In research on how students felt about belonging as they transitioned into higher education, they found:

> The negative thoughts took different forms in each individual, of course, but they mostly gathered around two ideas. One set of thoughts was about belonging. Students in transition often experienced profound doubts about whether they really belonged—or could ever belong—in their new institution. The other was connected to ability. Many students believed in what Carol Dweck had named an entity theory of intelligence—that intelligence was a fixed quality that was impossible to improve through practice or study. And so when they experienced cues that might suggest that they weren't smart or academically able—a bad grade on a test, for instance—they would often interpret those as a sign that they could never succeed. Doubts about belonging and doubts about ability often fed on each other, and together they created a sense of helplessness. That helplessness dissuaded students from taking any steps to change things.[14]

As we prepare students in our classrooms to be proficient communicators in world language, they are immersed in "otherness"—other language, other culture, new tasks that they have never attempted. Is your class a place students belong? When they meet those early challenges, do you help them to see they have the ability to overcome them? Your classroom is the first step in preparing students to understand that we are all "others," and that we all belong and have value in our global communities.

We also have to make the connection that just as we compare our home culture to that of other countries, daily we compare our own culture to that of other classes, races, religions, or ethnicities. Just as we may view visitors from other countries as "others," we also perceive otherness in those of other skin colors, accents, abilities, gender or sexual identities, even forms of dress. We may not be cognizant of this comparison on a day-to-day basis,

14   Tough, P. (2014, May 15). Who gets to graduate? The New York Times Magazine. Retrieved from https://www.nytimes.com/2014/05/18/magazine/who-gets-to-graduate.html

but language is an important determiner of "otherness." How you express yourself can determine whether others consider you worthy of a certain grade, job, or social group.

Part of our role as language educators is to make students aware that their voice is valuable. For students of privilege, who may not understand that the voices of others are as important as theirs, help them explore those voices and come to understand their value. For students who may hear messages that they are less valuable, help them to understand their inherent worth and the importance of advocacy. As a matter of preparation for the world beyond the classroom, we must consider both students' vision for themselves, as well as a vision of success for them. If we know that success in higher education opens doors of opportunity for stability and comfort, then meeting students' immediate needs, equipping them with the tools to succeed, and instilling in them the belief that they can succeed are necessary parts of our role as educators.

More than once when preparing a common assessment for my district, a language educator looked at me with serious concern and said, "My (impoverished) students can't do what those (affluent) students can." My question is why not? Certainly they have equal capacity for learning as students in affluent schools. Do you believe that all your students can and should achieve with language? Do you understand how language is important to the lives of all your students? Do you have the tools to show them how their life connects to lives around the globe all day every day? Do you believe their lives are as important as the lives of others across the globe? I do.

Teachers equip students with the language and understanding to navigate their current realities and to be ready to take on future opportunities and challenges.

BIG IDEAS

It's easy to forget that content is designed, rather than prescribed, much like it's easy to overlook our students' goals as we push towards standards. If we (students and teachers) are truly going to achieve a quality result, we have to connect learners to rich, relevant, contextualized content and then empower them to use it, to see themselves as part of the stories we tell.

Questions for Reflection

1. What is one way you "de-skilled" a task or assessment recently? What is one change you could make to that task to allow students to exceed the prescribed boundaries of learning?
2. What is an authentic source that you have used or could use to address a content standard, and which is rich in interdisciplinary historical context (geography, politics, art, etc.)?
3. Think about a content standard that you know students will struggle to connect with. What other design quality could you leverage to deliver that content in a way that students will find engaging?
4. The gut response to "Is your class a place all students belong?" is, of course, yes. In reality though, we know there are students, or kinds of students, that we struggle to connect to—personally or academically. Who is that in your room, and how can you begin to address your own assumptions and actions (because that is all you have control of) so that those students get the profound benefit of the quality intellectual work you design?

ORGANIZATION OF KNOWLEDGE

Knowledge is clear and accessible by nature of
the way it is presented or discovered

LET US START by differentiating between knowledge and information. Information exists in the world. Knowledge is information that has been internalized for use by an individual. In world languages, we'll refer to knowledge in terms of proficiency because it represents the degree to which a student can use information. To guide students to knowledge, we must open a door for growth, clearly lay out the steps or path that results in growth, and provide students opportunities to access or discover, and then internalize information.

Before we tackle student tasks, teachers need a clear picture of how content, standards, design qualities, and proficiency interrelate. As you look at the graphic on the next page, consider your own design process and what elements you share with the pictured model. Consider areas that differ or are missing from your own process and how that may influence student proficiency.

Our overarching goal is proficiency, and it is what we will assess. Our assessment will be refined to the context of the theme of a unit of study. For each unit, essential questions will guide our exploration of content. As we explore and interact with content, the activities we do will reflect the design qualities and modes of language.

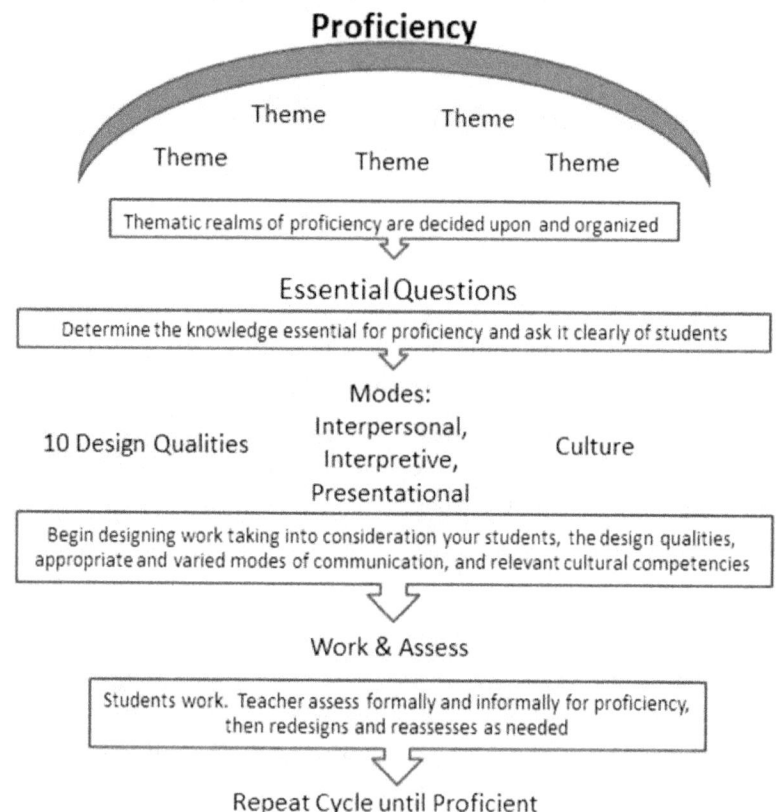

Proficiency

Theme   Theme

Theme   Theme   Theme

Thematic realms of proficiency are decided upon and organized

Essential Questions

Determine the knowledge essential for proficiency and ask it clearly of students

Modes:
10 Design Qualities   Interpersonal,   Culture
Interpretive,
Presentational

Begin designing work taking into consideration your students, the design qualities, appropriate and varied modes of communication, and relevant cultural competencies

Work & Assess

Students work. Teacher assess formally and informally for proficiency, then redesigns and reassesses as needed

Repeat Cycle until Proficient

Planning for Proficiency: Models

It can be difficult to juggle content standards, resources, and learning strategies while meeting proficiency targets in different communicative modes while highlighting cultural context. That's a big job! If you're trying to find a place to start, I encourage you to consider a template like mine below. In addition to the blank template, I've included samples for a novice and an advanced secondary-level course. On the samples, I have circled what I considered to be the primary design qualities. Depending on the details of the work, other qualities may also be present, or you may find ways to connect to those qualities with similar or additional tasks. As you review student engagement in work, it may help you to revisit the design qualities of work on which they have been most engaged. It may also help you to identify your own preferences for design. For example, I tend to prefer lessons with a high level of affiliation, novelty, and variety. For students who prefer organization and quiet, individual work, my classroom poses a high level of risk for learning, and I sacrifice their engagement (and consequently content mastery) by not balancing their work with adequate tasks in which they prefer to engage. Being aware of my own preferences helps me be a better designer for my students.

Learner Proficiency Level:	Unit Theme:
Elaborates on a variety of topics with cultural and situational awareness. Comprehends extended discussion. Can be understood by a speaker who is unaccustomed to language learners. *Advanced* Participates in brief conversation by using strings of sentences and combining phrases to form original ideas. Can be understood by a sympathetic listener. *Intermediate* Manages limited words & phrases. Answers simple questions. Difficult to understand. *Novice*	**Essential/Guiding Questions:**

Knowledge Work

	Interpersonal	Presentational	Interpretive
Oral & Aural			
Design Qualities	AFL AFM ATH ORG RSK CH PR NV CT ST	AFL AFM ATH ORG RSK CH PR NV CT ST	AFL AFM ATH ORG RSK CH PR NV CT ST
Text & Print			
Design Qualities	AFL AFM ATH ORG RSK CH PR NV CT ST	AFL AFM ATH ORG RSK CH PR NV CT ST	AFL AFM ATH ORG RSK CH PR NV CT ST

Design Qualities Key:

RSK = Protection from Risk/Initial Failure   NV = Novelty & Variety   CH = Choice
ORG = Organization & Structure   ATH = Authenticity   AFM = Affirmation
CT = Content & Substance   PR = Product Focus   AFL = Affiliation
ST = Clear and Compelling Standards

The first step to organization of knowledge is the organization of thematic units. As the unit's work is planned, it is necessary that it be done in a way that answers the essential questions of the unit and results in proficiency. Now that we have a map and models for unit design, let's take a look at some tools to give day-to-day tasks some consistency in organization and structure. I have shown directions here in English but would present them in the target language in the classroom. Students can still work with a strong level of autonomy, or choice, for leveled, inductive activities. Remember, one of our assumptions about Working on the Work is that the teacher's role is one of an expert facilitator and students are knowledge workers. The teacher orients students toward the tools and clues, then provides structure and feedback so that students can work to link the tools and clues in a way that results in learning. Choice is a good way to engage students in inductive work. The way that you organize choices with graphic organizers, sequenced steps, and carefully culled realia is what gives structure to learning. Let's examine several models for lending structure to assignments with a high level of autonomy. Each set will address the same thematic topic from the perspective of novice, intermediate, and advanced proficiency.

Learner Proficiency Level:	Unit Theme:

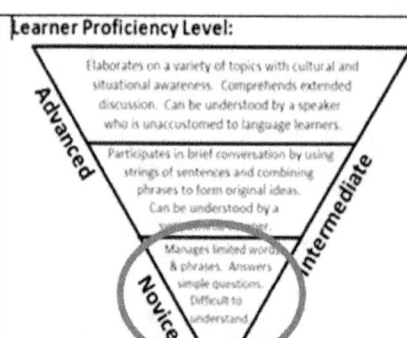

Elaborates on a variety of topics with cultural and situational awareness. Comprehends extended discussion. Can be understood by a speaker who is unaccustomed to language learners.

Participates in brief conversation by using strings of sentences and combining phrases to form original ideas. Can be understood by a...

Manages limited words & phrases. Answers simple questions. Difficult to understand.

Advanced / Intermediate / Novice

Unit Theme:

My Family & I

Essential/Guiding Questions:

-Who is part of a family?
-What does your family look like?
-What does your family like to do?

	Knowledge Work		
	Interpersonal	Presentational	Interpretive
Oral & Aural	Interview a classmate about his/her family. Answer your partner's questions about your family.	Present your favorite family member to the class. Tell how they are related to you and describe their appearance & likes.	-Watch a news broadcast about the royal family. Next to the name, tell the role of the family member. -Listen to a native speaker describe her family. Fill in her family tree as she talks.
Design Qualities	(AFL) AFM (ATH) ORG RSK (CH) PR (NV) CT ST	AFL AFM (ATH) ORG RSK (CH) PR NV CT ST	AFL AFM ATH ORG (RSK) AFL AFM ATH ORG PR (NV) CT (ST)
Text & Print	Write a letter to your pen pal describing your family and asking him about his.	Trace a family tree for yourself or a famous family, labeling the role of at least 6 family members. Illustrate it with drawings or photos.	Read the table about family size in the target counties and respond to questions about the data.
Design Qualities	AFL (AFM) (ATH) ORG RSK CH (PR) NV CT ST	AFL AFM ATH (ORG) RSK CH PR NV (CT) ST	AFL AFM ATH (ORG) RSK CH PR NV CT ST

Design Qualities Key:

RSK = Protection from Risk/Initial Failure
ORG = Organization & Structure
CT = Content & Substance
ST = Clear and Compelling Standards

NV = Novelty & Variety
ATH = Authenticity
PR = Product Focus

CH = Choice
AFM = Affirmation
AFL = Affiliation

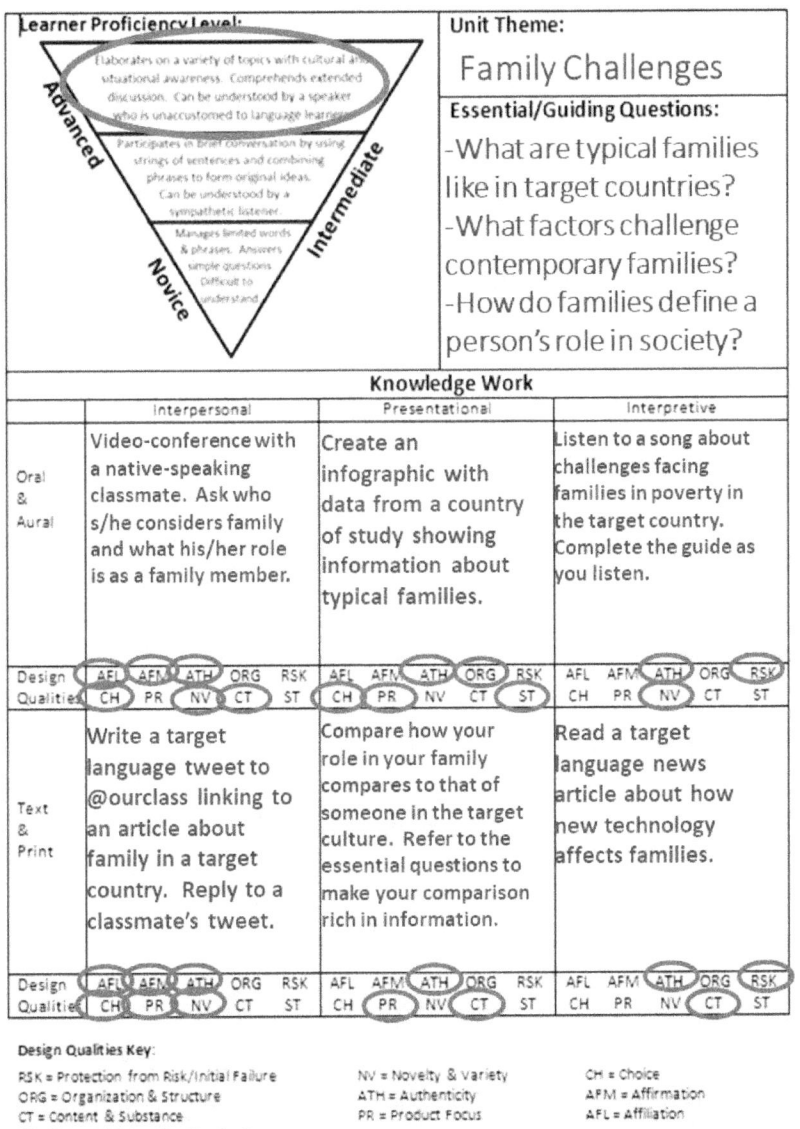

Learner Proficiency Level:			Unit Theme:		
Advanced: Elaborates on a variety of topics with cultural and situational awareness. Comprehends extended discussion. Can be understood by a speaker who is unaccustomed to language learners. *Intermediate*: Participates in brief conversation by using strings of sentences and combining phrases to form original ideas. Can be understood by a sympathetic listener. *Novice*: Manages limited words & phrases. Answers simple questions. Difficult to understand.			**Family Challenges**		
			Essential/Guiding Questions:		
			-What are typical families like in target countries? -What factors challenge contemporary families? -How do families define a person's role in society?		
Knowledge Work					
	Interpersonal		Presentational		Interpretive
Oral & Aural	Video-conference with a native-speaking classmate. Ask who s/he considers family and what his/her role is as a family member.		Create an infographic with data from a country of study showing information about typical families.		Listen to a song about challenges facing families in poverty in the target country. Complete the guide as you listen.
Design Qualities	~~AFL~~ ~~AFM~~ ~~ATH~~ ORG RSK ~~CH~~ PR ~~NV~~ CT ST		~~AFL~~ AFM ~~ATH~~ ~~ORG~~ RSK ~~CH~~ ~~PR~~ NV CT ~~ST~~		AFL AFM ~~ATH~~ ORG ~~RSK~~ CH PR ~~NV~~ CT ST
Text & Print	Write a target language tweet to @ourclass linking to an article about family in a target country. Reply to a classmate's tweet.		Compare how your role in your family compares to that of someone in the target culture. Refer to the essential questions to make your comparison rich in information.		Read a target language news article about how new technology affects families.
Design Qualities	~~AFL~~ ~~AFM~~ ~~ATH~~ ORG RSK ~~CH~~ ~~PR~~ ~~NV~~ CT ST		AFL ~~AFM~~ ~~ATH~~ ORG RSK ~~CH~~ ~~PR~~ NV ~~CT~~ ST		AFL AFM ~~ATH~~ ~~ORG~~ ~~RSK~~ CH PR NV ~~CT~~ ~~ST~~

Design Qualities Key:

RSK = Protection from Risk/Initial Failure	NV = Novelty & Variety	CH = Choice
ORG = Organization & Structure	ATH = Authenticity	AFM = Affirmation
CT = Content & Substance	PR = Product Focus	AFL = Affiliation
ST = Clear and Compelling Standards		

Organizing Inductive Learning

The first step to organization of knowledge is the organization of thematic units. As the unit's work is planned, it is necessary that it be done in a way that answers the essential questions of the unit and results in proficiency. Now that we have a map and models for unit design, let's take a look at some tools to give day-to-day tasks some consistency in organization and structure. I have shown directions here in English but would present them in the target language in the classroom. Students can still work with a strong level of autonomy, or choice, for leveled, inductive activities. Remember, one of our assumptions about Working on the Work is that the teacher's role is one of an expert facilitator and students are knowledge workers. The teacher orients students toward the tools and clues, then provides structure and feedback so that students can work to link the tools and clues in a way that results in learning. Choice is a good way to engage students in inductive work. The way that you organize choices with graphic organizers, sequenced steps, and carefully culled realia is what gives structure to learning. Let's examine several models for lending structure to assignments with a high level of autonomy. Each set will address the same thematic topic from the perspective of novice, intermediate, and advanced proficiency.

Inductive Learning Thematic Example A:
My Class Schedule (Scaffolding Organization with Choice)
Earlier in the chapter on choice, we looked at a guided conversation. The more proficient your student, the less guidance they will need, but you can scaffold their learning with level-appropriate guides. Let's revisit that guided conversation with a similar task. At each proficiency level, students are asked to make choices and give opinions about their classes. The way that they are asked to express themselves is structured according to proficiency level. At the lowest level, a graphic organizer helps students clearly see how content is related and make choices for communication. For intermediate students, simple guided questions and clear directions provide just enough tools for a student to comprehend what is asked and respond appropriately. At the end of the intermediate task, students are asked to briefly synthesize the information they have gathered. Advanced students have the least structural support, but their expected product is clearly communicated and is driven by content which students will find compelling—the quality of their classes and the opinions of their peers.

Novice

My first class is		We use a		The class is		
✓	Math	✓	calculator			boring
✓	Science	✓	book	✓		fun
	Literature	✓ ✓	paper	✓	✓	interesting
✓	History	✓	pen/pencil	✓		good

Find three colors. Speak to three people. Read the sentence below, choosing words to make the sentence complete. Record information about your partners by marking in the color that represents them.

Red = Jacque, Black = Josephine, Blue = Marie

Intermediate

The office is talking about switching you into a different first-period class. Ask 3-5 friends about their classes to get an idea of your options. Find out:

- What class do you have first period?
- What materials do you need?
- How is the class?

Record their responses and conclude your notes by writing which alternate first period you would choose and why.

Advanced

Speak with your group mates about their favorite classes. Come to a consensus on what classes you recommend for a new student and why. Be prepared to present your suggested schedule with the rationale to be voted upon by your classmates.

Inductive Learning Thematic Example B:
Developing Vocabulary for the Home (Organizing Input)
In these thematic tasks about the home, students are directed to content and asked questions that connect to prior learning in order to scaffold the

construction of new knowledge. The novice task gives students the freedom to explore unfiltered content and connect with the language in multiple ways. It assumes that students can figure out information on their own, and, in doing so, affirms to the students that the teacher trusts and believes in them. It also validates their interests by asking students to direct learning with their own questions. The intermediate task assumes that students have some prior knowledge of the home but opens the door for students to use language that they find while browsing to describe specific elements that suit their interests. It also asks students to connect their culture to that of target cultures. In the advanced task, comparing and contrasting homes is a task that is at once extremely comfortable and extremely profound. It questions their own experience but also connects it deeply with the homes of their peers in other countries. While students will develop advanced proficiency because of what they are asked to write, the advancement will be driven by their curiosity to discover a genuine answer, and be based on authentic, contemporary realia.

Novice

10 Words You . . .

Recognize (cognates or learned before)	Figured Out (from context or with a dictionary)	Would like to Know (they're repeated a lot or about a topic you find interesting)
1.	1.	1.

Google the term "home design magazine" (in the target language). Browse the first two or three links and make a list of the following:

Intermediate

Google the term "home design magazine" (in the target language). Browse the first two or three links and answer the following in sentences:

- How is an "ideal home" described in the magazine?
- What rooms or things can be found in an "ideal home?"
- Name three ways your home is similar to or different from the homes you see.

Advanced

Google three home design magazines from different target countries. Answer the following in paragraph form, drawing connections between what you see in the magazines:

- What are some unique characteristics that set each country's home design apart from one another?
- What are some common characteristics among the homes you see and read about?
- What can you infer about the practices and perspectives of the countries based on the similarities and differences between them?

Inductive Grammar Model

Many teachers find it extremely difficult to develop students' understanding of structure without diverting learning from context and presenting overt grammar rules. Some students are driven by rules and formulae and need to have them for comprehension, but that does not mean that rules need to be taught explicitly by the teacher. Consider the following narrative about how two of my colleagues approached grammar instruction differently:

> In a unit with a new verb tense, "Mrs. Estructura" gives notes on the verb endings, reinforces the endings by asking students to complete a verb conjugation worksheet and then participate in a conjugation board game. To conclude, she asks students to fill in the blanks on a quiz with the appropriate verb form for the subject given. The students do well at conjugating verbs because they can follow patterns and match pairs, but some students can't tell you what the forms mean or who does the actions.

> For the same unit, "Mr. Decouver" revisits subject pronouns and some previously studied infinitives and narrates about the people in his day. He tells about the activities they do in the target language using pictures, gestures, and students to help act out his story. He asks questions in the target language about who does what,

and students answer him, recycling the information they used. Mr. Decouver follows up by giving them a comic strip, where he has written the text from his story in the boxes. Students illustrate the actions, showing who does what. To conclude, the teacher gives students a conjugation organizer and asks students to fill in the verb endings based on what they've heard and draw conclusions about how to use verbs to tell what happens. The following day, students create their own comic strip telling what people in their day do.

Both teachers taught students to use verb endings. Mrs. Estructura started by presenting the explicit rules and then asked students to follow them. Mr. Decouver guided his students to the rules by organizing materials and work in a way that engaged students and asked questions that forced them to organize their own knowledge. Like Mrs. Estructura, Mr. Decouver assessed student knowledge, but his product was one that was authentic to student interests (talking about themselves) and connected with deep knowledge. Students were expected to make their own connections, rather than parrot patterns and match terms. The work designed by Mr. Decouver acknowledged students' abilities and experiences and honored them by expecting profound learning to be a result thereof.

Rather than look at a thematic task in the task samples that follow, we will look at a structural task: giving commands. Like the other inductive learning models in this chapter, you will see a novice, intermediate, and advanced proficiency task, each elaborating students' ability to interpret and produce commands in the target language.

Novice

Take a look at the advertisements your group has been provided. In your group, make a list of verbs as they are used in the ads. Draw some assumptions about those verbs based on these considerations:

- Where and how are the verbs used?
- Are there any similarities in verb form?

- Based on what you know about advertisements, and about the meaning of the words in these ads, what can you infer about the reason for using this verb form?

Intermediate

	Meme	Comic	Video
List the commands as the moms use them	1. 2. 3. 4.	1. 2. 3. 4. 5.	1. 2. 3.
How do the command forms change from the beginning to the end of the source?			
What rules can you infer about using commands or direct object pronouns?			

Using your devices, scan the links to the meme, comic, and video in which moms order their children to do chores. Complete the guide as you watch/read:

Advanced

Step 1: Watch the commercial for the appliance outlet and answer the questions:

- What tasks does the wife ask her husband to do? How does the husband respond?
- What does the husband do? How do you think this ad is or is not effective for selling appliances?
- Who is the intended audience of the commercial?
- What inferences can we make about the practices or perspectives of the target country based on this commercial?

Step 2: Think of a situation in which someone has told you to do something that you didn't want to do. Sketch the conversation in the comic strip below showing what you were told, how you responded, and the end result of the exchange.

Organizing Cultural Knowledge of Products, Practices, and Perspectives

Part of proficiency in global communication is our ability to navigate language through the lens of understanding of the speaker. While the language task will vary from level to level, students at any level can identify and connect products, practices, and perspectives of target cultures. Let's take Valentine's Day as an example. In the USA, the products would include items like cards, boxed chocolates, and heart decorations. The practices would include exchanging Valentines in grade school, gifting candy to a loved one, or going on a romantic date with a sweetheart. You could infer that these things represent an American perspective that it is important to celebrate love, or that we show that we love someone by giving them candy. As we come across an example of product, practice, or perspective in the realia we use, we can train students to put that piece in the global context from which it arises. Therefore, if a teacher of English language learners were to use a Valentine's chocolate advertisement for a unit about describing food, the next step after accessing the language and structures of the ad would be to ask questions about the purpose of the ad or what American practices and perspectives it represents. Develop a simple graphic organizer to use throughout the course such as the one below to help students organize their learning. As you approach new culture questions, compare them to information students already know to build depth using prior knowledge.

As we design work for learning, we help students engage with authentic materials by scaffolding with prior knowledge and guiding questions. In an effort to keep culture multidimensional, we ask students to step out of the typical textbook culture box and give structure to cultural understanding through the comparison of products, practices, and perspectives. In these ways, we not only communicate and organize content, but we also help students reflect on the process of building meaning with language.

Compare the American holidays of Valentines Day and Halloween

Topic:	Valentine's	Halloween
Products:	*Candy, Cards, Heart Decorations*	*Candy, Treat sacks, Costumes, Scary decorations*
Practices:	*Exchange candy and cards, dress up for a romantic date*	*Give away candy to trick-or-treaters, Dress up in scary costume, Go to a haunted house*
Perspectives:	*-Love is important to celebrate* *-Red is a symbol for love* *-Giving loved ones candy is a way to show you care* *-Valentine's is celebrated with loved ones* *-Inspired by a saint*	*- Scaring people is fun* *- Costume play is fun* *- It's ok to ask for and give candy to strangers on Halloween* *- Neighborhoods support children* *-Rooted in pagan and religious institutional beliefs about fall, harvest, and death*

Conclusions: *Many American holidays celebrate with candy. Many American holidays are celebrated more by children. Many American holidays are rooted in Christian tradition.*

BIG IDEAS

When we defined "Organization of Knowledge" at the start of this chapter, we posited that "knowledge is clear and accessible by nature of the way it is presented or discovered." As much as possible, students should drive their own learning. The knowledge students discover has a greater impact on learning than the information that they are presented with. Further, inductive learning builds confidence and affirms work, so students stay more deeply engaged. My vocabulary and grammar examples don't begin with explicit instruction by a teacher. Rather, the approach is more Socrative, where the teacher scaffolds students' exposure to resources with targeted questions to help them coax out and organize important information on their own. Without the graphic organizers and scaffolded questions, students would be overwhelmed by the quantity of information and unable to organize it for building meaning. Likewise, specific realia was paired with a targeted task that guided students to comprehension and production. Inductive learning opens many doors to allow for student choice, to affirm a student's ability to find and use information, and to create an authentic language product of importance to the student. By teaching in a way that encourages students to find and organize meaning, we can also teach them to question cultural practices, products, and perspectives. When we embed the search for meaning in authentic materials, we maintain the inherent global context of our source and create an opportunity for students to make connections between language, location, and history.

Questions for Reflection

Think of an authentic source you have used recently:

1. What thematic vocabulary is embedded in your source?
2. What grammatical concept(s) are embedded in (native to) your source?
3. With what embedded cultural similarities or differences can your students make a connection?
4. What course-level-appropriate questions could you ask your students that would guide them to find those answers themselves?

AFFIRMATION

When "significant others" affirm that your work is important

CLASS WORK WILL bring students into contact with peers, teachers, family, and the community. "Community" may imply local residents, or it may extend to internet communities and social networks. Whether or not work has an audience beyond the student and his teacher, students will hear feedback regularly about their work and the quality of their products. In the classroom, peers comment on how a student speaks or writes. In school or via social media, students will comment about assignments and their value by saying things like, "We're doing a cool game today," or "Did you do the project? It took forever and I don't even want to present it." Teachers, of course, also respond to the quality of student products, giving feedback in the form of comments or grades. Parents may hear or see student work if it is a necessary part of a task, or if the student chooses to share it with his parent. As students chat, blog, read, or post on social networks, they know immediately if they have been understood or if they understand. If work takes students into the community, then citizens, newspapers, and leaders comment on the products of their work. At any and all of these levels, others tell students whether or not their work is good and if it matters.

DOES THIS WORK MATTER TO THE PEOPLE WHO MATTER?

So, is the work you design good and does it matter? If the answer is "YES!" then your students will likely receive a lot of affirmation. If the answer isn't "Yes," then you need to rethink the work you give to students. If work matters because not doing it results in a zero, that's probably not a very good reason. If work matters because doing it results in a 100, that's probably not a very good reason, either. What does a student stand to get out of a task? What ability or product are they going to take home tonight that they can use, and is that product compelling enough for them to want to get it? These questions of knowledge and product are critical when it comes to affirmation. If a parent doesn't understand or see the value in student work, he can never affirm its value to his child. The more people you connect with through the work you ask of students, the more opportunities students have to hear affirmation that their work is important. If the only person ever exposed to student work is the student's teacher, then the student never has the chance to hear from the world outside her classroom that her work is relevant to the world.

Once you've asked yourself some tough, but fundamental questions about whether the work you design has value outside the classroom, and who the work's target audience is, next you must actively listen to your students to find out who they consider to be "significant others." Some will depend on feedback from their peers. Those who thrive on class participation, or who are first to volunteer to put their poster in the hall, or the first to respond to a class blog post may hold the affirmation of their peers and teacher in high regard. Those who ask to take a copy of their graded paper home to show parents or who tell stories of using the content at home with their family will be particularly engaged if a task results in parent involvement or feedback. Others may not care much for classroom, or even parental feedback, but may be moved by service to their community or by community recognition, such as being featured or published in a periodical. Many have thriving digital lives and may seek affirmation from their digital colleagues about the work they do.

Outside of the work and words teachers offer to engage students in work, it is also important to give students opportunities for affirmation from people other than the teacher or their classmates. Involve students in work that connects with those people and things that are important to them. Affirmation is another way to make learning authentic. When you can show that content really does connect with the lives of people they care about, then you help students connect with content. Whether or not a student values your content, if the people they care about find value in it, students will engage in work to earn the affirmation of their loved ones. While your class products are tied to content, it is not the only quality that "significant others" may value. Qualities such as authenticity, product focus, or novelty may be what catches the attention of students' loved ones. Let's say students are making a brief oral presentation about their family in which they describe three family members using a visual. Most parents value family and enjoy showing others about their family through pictures. This task is authentic to them and very relatable. Consequently, parents may invest time in the student's work by helping find pictures or creating a visual. They may ask to hear a student's presentation. By showing that the work is valuable enough for their time and attention, even students who don't have a burning intrinsic desire to tell others what their siblings look like will engage in the content long enough to create the product that their parents attend to. Likewise, if students were asked to demonstrate the meaning of emotions with a music montage, their peers may have a high level of interest in what songs their classmates pair with a vocabulary term. Just as talking about family is authentic to parents, expressing emotion through music is authentic to students, and the process of creating an original musical product holds high value in society. The value their peers and society place on their unique music montage product may lead some students to a deeper level of engagement where they carefully evaluate how songs represent content terms. For students who place a high value on involvement with the community, attending local events tied to the target language or culture, volunteering with or for the benefit of target communities, or even creating a language product that can be used in their community may be work that results in affirmation for students that the content they're studying is important and useful in their lives.

Do students know their work matters to you?

The first and foremost source of affirmation for students is teachers. Part of what makes affirmation so integral is its close relationship with risk. "Does the teacher affirm that I can achieve?" If that essential question is not met with a vote of confidence, students think twice about whether or not they're willing to risk themselves with work that will never result in affirmation. When we reframe a student's grade to align with proficiency and growth, we empower students to drive their own success. Rather than how many questions a student got right on the last test (which is irrelevant compared to the one before), students begin to ask themselves questions like, "What kinds of things do I need to learn to take my proficiency to the next level?" Instead of acquiring points, they focus on acquiring skills. If we add in a growth component, we place even more value on the student's ability to master new content. Should a student who enters a third-year language course at an Intermediate-high proficiency and leaves at the same proficiency be given the same grade as a student who enters at Novice-Mid and leaves Intermediate-High? I believe it is necessary to assess and affirm growth so that students have a clear purpose for learning. If a student enters our room and leaves with no tangible evidence of growth, then the teacher hasn't designed work in a way that led him to it. The teacher has either failed to design work that engaged the student, failed to present relevant content, or failed to assess and give feedback in a way that resulted in growth. When we design work that engages students, we affirm their learning more than any verbal or written "Way to go!" ever could.

BIG IDEAS

Two of the major indicators of engagement center around whether students find work personally meaningful and whether students believe that doing the work will accomplish something of worth. The affirmation of others in response to their work is what makes it meaningful, whether those others are family, friends, or community. The teacher-student relationship is central to engagement and learning and is what allows the teacher to design to meet the student's needs and motivates the student to seek the teacher's affirmation. If your students aren't responding to your affirmation, you may need to invest in your relationship.

Questions for Reflection

1. Who is it easy to affirm? How do I show them affirmation?
2. Who do I struggle to affirm? How can I show them more affirmation?
3. Who is the target audience of the work my students do? Do they have an audience besides just the teacher?
4. What opportunities do I create for students to receive meaningful affirmation from people that matter to them?

AFFILIATION

Working interdependently

I PLAY A game with my students that we call "Trashketball." We use the recycling bin as a basket and set up three lines for throwing the ball—one worth 100 points, the next worth 200 points, and the third worth 300 points. I'll put the first sentence on the board, usually a relatively simple one that hits on major vocabulary and structures from the unit. Next, I direct student teams to write the sentence on a handheld whiteboard. The catch is that team members must construct the sentence one person at a time. Each team member may write or change one word, then they must pass it to the next person. When they think they're through, they show me their answer to check for correctness. Whoever has the board when the sentence is complete (and correct) will make three shots from whichever locations they choose. As soon as a correct statement is shown to me, I add the next statement to the board. As teams correctly show me each sentence, they take their shots and tally their points. To earn points, several things have to happen:

1. team members have to communicate, collaborate, and share knowledge
2. team members have to work quickly
3. individuals have to successfully shoot a ball into a basket

Therefore, even if a team happens to have all the "smart people" on it, if they can't make a basket or collaborate to create meaning, it's likely they will lose. The team relies on each individual to be an expert in the construction of meaning, as well as making a basket, so that the team has an opportunity to earn points. This reliance on one another is affiliation. Their success is interwoven with the unique skills and abilities each member brings to the task. While the use of points often drives students in point-based games, I find that with this game, most students get so caught up in the process that they often don't even care about the scores of other teams— further evidence that it is the affiliation that engages them, and not the product.

Putting students on a team doesn't mean they will rely on one another or work interdependently. For example, I recently paired students in differenti- ated groups based on a writing proficiency assessment. I expected students to collaborate on their work using their unique strengths and focusing on eliminating common weaknesses. However, the goal of the task was simply to revise and improve their work, and many students chose to work in silence next to their partner, and instead ask questions to me or to friends they knew better. They completed the task, but since interdependence was not required, students focused on their product.

PART OF SOMETHING BIGGER

An easy way to impose affiliation is by assigning team members to sort them- selves into roles within a group. For example: "In our activity today you'll be making a video of friends ordering food in a restaurant. For the video, you'll need two friends, one waiter, and one videographer." I've seen other teachers attempt to make students accountable for affiliation by assigning a common product, but with individual tasks. The teacher will say something like, "Your group is going to make a presentation about ordering food in a restaurant. One person will make a menu with food from your country. One person will convert the menu prices into target country currency and pro- vide visuals for the foods. One person will write a target language dialogue in which a patron orders food from a waiter. Your project is due Friday." Although the "team" will turn in their papers stapled together, they each have an individual job, for which interdependence is not required. If the teacher makes the team's grade dependent on the participation of the three individu- als, that may motivate some students to produce quality work, but for those students for whom grades and content are unimportant, there will be some unhappy and overworked team-mates. If the product requires collaboration (as in the first example), the students working on it will form groups that reflect the number of people required to complete the task. They will organize themselves according to their skills. In the case of the restaurant video skit, at its beginning, students with a high level of risk or a limited engagement in content were often eager to volunteer for the role of videographer. However, if their peers found that they didn't understand what or how to film in a way that told their story, the teams would reorganize so that all teammates played an effective role in a successful product. Likewise, students eager to be on camera, but who struggled with demonstrating content were often redirected behind the camera. Students recognized that proficiency at the task was a product of working together in a way that made the most of their skills and knowledge. They each played a part in a task that was bigger than any one of them had the tools to complete.

FILLING THE GAP

Although these early examples require a full class period or more to complete, tasks with a high level of affiliation need not consume as much time. Quick guided pair conversations can easily be completed in around ten minutes. To turn conversations into an activity with affiliation, ask students to gather information from peers as they work. These types of activities are known as "Info Gap" activities. Let's look at a few examples:

1. You work for mall security and your partner's family member has gone missing. Ask your partner to describe his relative. As he describes him/her, draw a quick sketch according to his description. When he's done, show him your picture to verify before you post the picture to your colleagues.

2. You're a journalist doing an article about how your hometown is attracting people from around the nation and the world. Survey the locals and find out where people are from. Record your data and sum up 5 highlights for your editor to get the green light on the job.

3. It's your first time at the family reunion and you're trying to figure out who everyone is and how they are connected. Your class family can tell you their own names and 1-2 relations to help you place them on your family tree. Ask around until you have the tree complete. Suggestion: Use a famous family like the royals of Spain or the Weasleys of Harry Potter.

One of the critical components of these Info Gap activities is their connection to authentic scenarios. A missing person sketch, local interest news, and family trees are potential topics that students deal with on a day-to-day basis. Many textbook-issue Info Gap activities feature "Student A" and "Student B" pages that show a series of pictures and some "ask your partner" questions, such as "What's Susie wearing?" or "How does Bob feel?" While the questions address the grammar or vocab focus of the day, and require students to interact with one another to complete, they tend not to feature inherently motivating content. Who cares what Susie from the 1990's textbook has on? Whether or not my friend can use my description to make a sketch that actually looks like my mom is far more engaging. The more design qualities you can build into a task, the more likely you are to have a task that appeals to all students. By combining an affiliation-driven activity, with an authentic topic like finding out about classmates, or a product like a missing person's sketch, and then rolling the content in with clear standards for achievement, students can't help but be engaged.

Big Ideas

We all want to be needed, but we don't always feel that way. They may not say it, but students want you to need them, too! Do you (the teacher) and their classmates really need *them* to do the work? Is this a task any student can do, or does it matter that *this* student participates? When we design tasks in a way that students really are asked to bring their own skills and knowledge "to the job," they know others are depending on them and that they have something valuable to offer. So often teachers act like they're the primary source and director of learning, when really, it's the students who show up to and do the work. Affiliation is evidenced when students unite their work for a purpose outside of themselves, but which depends on each of their unique contributions to be fulfilled.

Questions for Reflection

1. Did you ever have a teaching moment when you thought, "I wish (specific student) was here for this activity"? Why did you feel that way? What was it about that student and that task that you knew they were meant for each other?

2. What kind of impact do you think it has on students when they're part of a learning environment where others need *them*, rather than where they need others?

3. Think of a group activity you've planned. What unique skills or knowledge does each group member provide to the work? Is there any member that doesn't have to bring something of their own to the task? If so, how could you rethink the roles in a way that every part is meaningful?

4. Let's return to that group activity in #3. What do group members get from each other that they want to know, rather than just what the teacher wants them to know?

Novelty and Variety

New forms of work and new products

I LOVE NOVELTY and variety. If I could do something new and exciting every day, I would. Novelty and variety keeps my students on their toes. How often is your students' first question, "Are we going to do something fun today." Yes, yes we are. We're playing the Hunger Games. We're going on a treasure hunt. We're becoming robot puppet masters. We're expressing our emotions through music. We're producing commercials for the school's morning news.

It's days like these that I tingle with anticipation and I'm pretty certain that my enthusiasm rubs off. However, not all of my students like to live on the edge. They remind me with comments like, "Do we have to play the review game? Can't we sit down and do a study guide?" These students are relieved by predictability and order, clear standards, and models for success. These students want to know how many points to get and how many questions there will be. So, as always, balance is the answer. Novelty and variety are engaging. They can also provoke new sensations, approach content through new modes of learning, and give students an opportunity for affirmation from and affiliation with students they don't work with every day. At the same time, students who find clear and compelling standards and organization of knowledge more important may struggle to find order and standards when they are asked to think outside the box. Either way, the teacher's goal is to help students connect with content and build proficiency.

In my experience, teachers don't struggle with organization and routines. A test every two weeks. Journal warm-ups every day. Definitions from the book and a puzzle worksheet at the start of every unit. Veteran teachers, in particular, have preferred activities that are comfortable and easy to prepare. I recognize that teachers will cultivate activities that suit their strengths; however, I also want you to remember that your strengths will not be the same as those of your students,' nor are you the person for whom the work is designed. The students are the knowledge workers. Let their learning drive the work you design and keep their engagement and proficiency needs at the forefront of your planning. That being said, here are a few suggestions for adding novelty and variety to your unit.

INCORPORATE POP CULTURE

Connect with the latest book, video game, hit song, movie, social media trend, etc. Use the characters' names in a dialogue or role play. Build a classroom game based on a plotline or videogame mission. Use the names or lyrics of students' favorite songs to build vocabulary. Use target language movie posters for contemporary movies. Use celebrities for the unit on comparisons (ex. Jay-Z is better/worse than Kanye West. Kim Kardashian has more/fewer husbands than Taylor Swift). By using contemporary culture to communicate content, you make the content relevant to today!

GET MOVING!

Changing seating arrangements is a superficial way to add novelty, but generally, it won't be appreciated unless it is done with purpose. Try rotating students through learning mode stations one day—arts/movement, writing, reading, speaking, listening—with activities for each mode from the current unit. Take students outdoors, to the hall, or to another open area for a language activity with movement. For example, cross to the other side of the hall if the statement applies to you (cross back on the next if the next one does, too). Play "Four corners" about likes and designate one corner each for "I don't like at all, I don't like, I like, and I like a lot." Have students move the corner that represents how they feel about a statement.

To incorporate movement on a smaller scale, toss a ball to students as you call on them, or have them stand as you review and, as each answers a question, have them sit one by one until all are seated. Invent an action for them to do as you review the vocabulary terms or use your body YMCA style for verb endings (we do pret-aerobics with the preterite verb endings!). Use individual whiteboards and have students hold up responses for quick feedback or pass boards for collaborative descriptions. Make class sets of vocabulary clip art to have students hold up, sort, or sequence. Bring props to support a unit that students must use to complete a task. For example, "dry your hair with the towel," "put the fork to the right of the plate," or "pick up the scarf and coat."

A LA MODE

For a large part of their day, a student's learning focuses on reading and writing. In world languages, we could add interpersonal speaking as a strong third, but we struggle to link language to other skills. Connecting language with other skills and subjects has the twofold benefit of opening avenues for learning for students who struggle with language because of a special need, or for enrichment for students who can take content above and beyond the confines of the standards. Here are a few examples for connecting with other modes of learning:

Mathematics

Use language for real-world math needs, like converting prices to stay within budget on a shopping trip or converting prices of products in an American store to the currencies of other countries as if you were their web designer preparing content for worldwide audiences. Use data from authentic charts and graphs to solve problems, answer questions, or make connections between target & native countries. The teachers of standardized subjects will thank you for using charts, graphs, and maps, and, if your course is part of a program that leads to AP, your students will be better prepared for AP content (and life!).

The Arts

Represent language with images, music, or video. Or, interpret images, music, and video into language. For example, watch a news program or short film once for content, then mute it and watch again, having students narrate or identify using the target language. Use or invent a song to teach a grammar point or vocabulary. Have a student percussionist drop a beat to use when reviewing content, call and response style. Bust out the playdough and ask students to represent content with a quick sculpt, rather than a sketch or a paragraph. Not all students are artists, but most appreciate art, and you will affirm those for whom art is a strength. Plus, any opportunity to get students to connect content with other realms of their lives is another opportunity to build knowledge and proficiency.

Logic & Games
Chunk vocabulary onto puzzle pieces and have students solve the language puzzle. Complete a task following a map or complete a map to follow a task. Use information to solve a logic puzzle (who's wearing what color shirt, or who's sitting where at the family reunion). Find a board game or game show template and modify it to suit your content.

Science & Technology
Scientific language is full of cognates, so it's easy to pick up an article or instructions and ask students of any level to work with the language of science. Further, the tools of technology are in the hands of our young people every day, and for many, following advances in science and technology is very engaging. Using tech tools for work is practical and authentic. It also affirms students because it recognizes their ability to find information for themselves. By allowing students to use their own tools and abilities for learning in places where they naturally live (ex. Those on Twitter, tweet. Those on YouTube, watch. Those on CNN or blogs, read.), we show students in a deep way how the target language connects with their day-to-day life. And, if your professional evaluator is checking, you're also differentiating instruction. I asked students the other day to pick 5 authentic tasks from a board of 15 choices. One of them was "Search a Twitter hashtag from the vocabulary of the unit. Write down the most interesting tweet." A student asked, "They make Twitter in Spanish?" They had never made the connection that people of other languages, perhaps living in other countries, are bumping around in their social spaces doing the same things they do. Most target-language technology articles measure in kilograms, kilometers, and degrees Celsius.

Students are always shocked that the rest of the world doesn't measure like them, and assuming the article is engaging enough, their next need is to know equivalents for those measurements. Suddenly, all their conversions in science and math are important all over again, and not just because they're on the test. Those "next steps," thinking about the tools they already use, but in a new, global way provides endless opportunities for novelty, and, more importantly, for empowering students to become students of the world, and in the world, rather than just in your classroom.

NOVEL PRODUCTS

Up to this point, most of our conversation has treated new forms of work. The other side of novelty and variety is new products. Now, if you're doing novel work, it's likely to have a novel product. However, it is also integral that proficiency be a product of all student work. In this sense, our product will never be entirely new, because it is always driven by content mastery. Nonetheless, students should have a variety of things to show for their work. Assuming our students are students "in the world," the way they present themselves to and interact with a target language audience serves as part of their product. Ask students to document their language products as proof of practice and proficiency. Let students set their own goals and find ways to meet them. When you expect students to rise to their goals, and you give them the support and tools they need to work, they will rise! Pick a simple format and follow up on student responses that don't appear to demonstrate growth. By allowing students a hand in designing their product, you can ensure that their work is engaging and their products are novel and varied.

To connect their products to proficiency, try having students organize and reflect on their products with a Portfolio. Assuming you're giving proficiency feedback, and they are organizing their work (either in the classroom or digitally), some questions like these should lead them to consider how they can develop their proficiency:

Sample Portfolio "Status Update" Questions and Responses

1. What was your last demonstrated proficiency point?

   I showed novice-high vocabulary.

2. What proficiency point does this product demonstrate?

   In this product, I show novice-high function and structure.

3. How does this product show growth?

   In my last sample, I used a lot of good new vocabulary, but I made a lot of grammatical mistakes that got in the way of communication. In this sample, I cleaned up my mistakes and used the right forms, so my function and structure and comprehensibility improved.

4. What is your next goal?

   I either want to demonstrate novice-high comprehension or bring my vocabulary up to intermediate-low.

5. What are some ways you can meet your next goal?

   I can do more journaling and find ways to expand my vocabulary about our unit. Or, I could do some of the listening modules from the Univ. of TX at Austin proficiency tasks.

6. By when do you plan to meet this goal?

   I think I can do this within a week. I plan to be done by next Friday.

BIG IDEAS

While some students thrive on organization and clear expectations, others need novelty and variety to keep them engaged. Knowing students well enough to know what's "trending" in their lives and incorporate it into their work is one way to keep activities fresh. If keeping up with the times isn't your forte, try mixing in movement, games, and connections to different academic subjects. For a truly novel experience, let students direct the paths of their own learning and determine the products that are worthy of evidence.

Questions for Reflection

Think of a common thematic unit you study with your students. Strategize how you can make the following connections between your unit and these areas:

1. What's trending in the news related to that unit of study?
2. What kind of physical movement is related to that unit of study?
3. What are two other school subjects that connect to that unit?
4. How could you ask your students to show proficiency that would result in unique products?

Engagement

Knowing exactly what is expected of you and
being compelled to demonstrate mastery

THE SCHLECHTY CENTER considers a student engaged when[15]:

1. The student sees the activity as personally meaningful.
2. The student's level of interest is sufficiently high that he persists in the face of difficulty.
3. The student finds the task sufficiently challenging that she believes she will accomplish something of worth by doing it.
4. The student's emphasis is on optimum performance and on "getting it right."

The purpose of Working on the Work is to engage students in learning. A deep understanding of the design qualities enables us to consider our students and our design in an attempt to create the optimum conditions for learning. I would argue that the design qualities apply to any work we do, not just the work of students in a classroom. For example, when my principal or my husband's region manager issues a policy and expects employees to follow it, the likelihood of the employees doing so will depend on whether employees have the support to make the change (Protection from Adverse Consequences), if they understand how to complete it (Clear and Compelling Standards), and if the change will benefit their unique situation (Authenticity). Your

---

15   Schlechty Center On Engagement. 1st ed. Schlechty Center, 2015. Web. 12 May 2015.

students are no different. So, if you have time constraints that prevent you from regularly speaking personally with your students (as I imagine you do), you need some tools to measure engagement and allow students ways to give you insightful feedback about whether or not you're succeeding at designing engaging work.

Most days I could look and listen and tell whether or not students were engaged, at least insofar as indicators 1, 2, and 4 are concerned. Average students will overcome challenges to understand and complete work. With support, encouragement, and a positive relationship with the teacher, they will seek to do work well and grow with affirmation. Authentic topics make work meaningful and exciting and help to build teacher-student trust that allows students to overcome difficulties in learning. Students trust the teacher, even when they don't entirely understand the value of their work. High functioning students rarely face difficulty mastering new content, and even the process of "figuring it out" is often affirmation enough to engage students.

Often, the greatest opportunity for increasing engagement lies in making sure the work you design has inherent worth. Let's run through a conversation that I often hear between teachers:

TEACHER 1: What are you doing today?

TEACHER 2: We're doing a vocab worksheet.

TEACHER 1: How's that going?

TEACHER 2: Good. The kids are getting it done. I let them listen to their music while they work.

TEACHER 1: What's next?

TEACHER 2: We'll do vocab worksheet #2 tomorrow to practice.

TEACHER 1: So how are you going to assess them?

TEACHER 2: I'll give them a quiz the next day. Assuming they could complete the blanks on the worksheet, they'll get a good grade. Then, we'll start the next topic.

In this situation, it appears the main item of worth is the grade. Students get feedback on presentational writing at the individual word level from the correct answer for the blank. Some will re-evaluate their incorrect answers, but they will likely never see those questions again, as the next assessment will assess the next topic. Many will simply file the grade away and begin to prepare themselves for the next unit. In this scenario, students probably engage long enough to earn a grade that meets their needs for affirmation or protection from adverse consequences, and others engage in listening to music. Their language proficiency feedback does not evaluate interpersonal or interpretive skills or cultural connections. The primary value students earn is a number grade on a transcript and minimally increased production in the target language, but they hardly develop skills that enable them to participate in a communicative exchange. To play devil's advocate for a moment, some of you will argue that the practice and refining of a structure (grammar) focus is integral to advancing proficiency. You're not wrong; however, this task has no evidence of any authentic content need (because cloze exercises are not authentic needs) with inherent value to a participant in a global world. And if your students are not being prepared for the world, what is your worth or role in their life? Sure, for some students increased proficiency (content knowledge) and a good grade (protection from adverse consequences) are enough to engage them in the task, but would you say that it's personally meaningful? Would you say that it includes challenging work and accomplishes something of worth in the world?

ASSESSING ENGAGEMENT

Engagement Survey
What did we do today?

Please check the box that best fits your answer:	Very much		Somewhat		Not much
	5	4	3	2	1
Did today's activities cause you to want to invest your time and energy to do them?					
Would you be willing to persist in this work even if you had difficulty with it?					
To what degree were you giving your time and energy the work because you <u>wanted to</u> do the work, rather than because you were looking to get a grade or avoid a consequence.					
Do you have any comments:					

There are lots of on-the-spot type engagement surveys, but many require students to identify themselves as they give feedback (raising a hand, holding a color). These do not address what I want most: unfiltered feedback from students with whom I didn't have much of a dialogue, and data so that I could approach engagement from an objective standpoint, rather than an "it felt great" standpoint. Here's a tool that I wrote to be time-efficient and effective at getting quality feedback:

I teach six world language classes per day. I set a box in the back of the room for engagement surveys, and throughout the day I try to remember to give out two in each class period. I aim for a variety of learners in each period: average, quiet, loud, gifted, special needs, eager, reluctant. I also make a point of asking for surveys from students I don't know as well, so I can build in extra opportunities for dialogue with them. The survey is anonymous, and I give them out discreetly, so there is no pressure on students from me or from peers as to their responses. Students place them in the box at the end of class, and periodically I assess the responses. Usually, I review them at the end of each unit, but occasionally I like to check them on a day when I try something new and want to know if it really worked or not.

The first question of the survey, "What did we do today?" tells me what the students got out of the work. Sometimes the answers showed a lot of depth ("we examined and shared news articles about the ecology of Spanish-speaking countries"), and sometimes they didn't ("we stood up and sat down"). I could often predict what kind of engagement scores I was likely to get after reading the responses to the first question.

The rating questions ask the respondent about doing the work. Notice that it never asks if s/he liked the work. It doesn't matter if work makes your student want to smile. Some of the best work I did was when I struggled, was fascinated, researched, and revised. It was not easy, and it did not make me smile until it was over and I had succeeded at reaching the product I was working for. Other work I struggled with, but only because my grade (and therefore my social life/allowance/college scholarship) depended on it. I cared about the benefits of the grade, not the benefits of the knowledge.

The last question, "Do you have any comments?" is the place where students will praise you, make suggestions for improvement, or occasionally suggest that you never do that again. For students who like to be nice, this is the place, since they couldn't do it in the ratings section, where students will give you a pat on the back. When I explain to students about the Engagement Surveys, I explain briefly what engagement means to me. Most students haven't thought about engagement beyond "I liked it," and the fact that I want to know if my work really engaged them builds a personal connection with students that helps them "lean in" when work really gets challenging because they trust I will make sure the results are worth it. I tell students that the surveys will be random and anonymous, but that if they would like to write their name they can (because a few always want to). I also tell them that their honest feedback matters to me, and that critical feedback is as valuable as positive because it lets me know how to design the best situations for learning.

For me, the engagement surveys were a good investment because:

1. It was nice to get affirmation. It doesn't happen often, and it makes me feel good.
2. The comments gave me quality suggestions for improvement and allowed me greater student insight than I had previously.
3. It felt good to honor the voices of all students equally. It's hard to do that every day in class, particularly with students who feel a high level of risk, either because of social constraints or academic ones. It was like giving students a golden ticket that said, "I care about how my class benefits you!"
4. DATA! Normally I'm a "play by feel" kind of person; however, once a unit (every 2-3 weeks on test day) I took the time to crunch the numbers (with some help calculating from my fast-finishers) and I was pleasantly surprised that my engagement data generally aligned with my assessment data. In fact, in my case, the averages were about half a percentage point apart. For me, it was pretty convincing evidence that the more I was able to engage my students, the greater their success could be on assessments.

Engagement surveys can be great, but if you want (or need) to start small, here are a few ideas:

- Put one of the rating questions on the board at the end of class and pass out post-its. Ask them to rate you and put the post-it on the door on the way out.
- Do a quick web survey via sites like Polleverywhere.com.
- Show a survey question and ask students to hold up the number of fingers that represent their response.

IF YOUR STUDENTS ARE NOT ENGAGED, WHAT THEN?

The number one complaint I hear from students in any classroom is "What does this have to do with my life?" If you use authentic, contemporary resources like music videos, games, news articles, work manuals, or even other students, then students can easily connect with these sources that they're already familiar with. For example, show a music video Beyoncé sings in other languages for her worldwide audiences. Ask students to interact with gamers to navigate a popular game in another's country's forum. Show them how current events from other countries connect with their own lives and histories and connect with the experiences of the immigrants and speakers of other languages already in your room. Make sure every day that students know that what they're doing is directly connected to their lives.

Know your students well enough to consider what design qualities engage them, and if you don't know them well enough, ask them. Then, build content-based activities around their feedback. Understand that what they consider important may not be what you consider important. Also, some variety is necessary to honor the interests and needs of all students. If you consistently rely on the same toolbox of activities, you will continually fail to serve students who don't or can't respond to those tools.

You may need to re-evaluate how you protect students from risk. If you often ask students to demonstrate proficiency in front of peers, or enforce set partner groups, students may feel too uncomfortable to practice or demonstrate proficiency. If your standards are not aligned with appropriate proficiency targets, students may struggle to meet them. Looking through some interpretive questions from one textbook, on every test students were expected to read and interpret information from sentences, strings of sentences, and passages. Students were asked to respond to multiple choice and short answer questions based on what they had read. According to the

ACTFL proficiency targets, a first-year novice-mid learner will understand some simple questions and statements and be able to produce a limited number of words, phrases, and sentences to provide basic information. If every test expects all students to correctly answer every question and use sentences for every short answer, it may not be correctly aligned with proficiency targets. Likewise, if you continue to expect the same kinds of answers in second- and third-year courses, your work is no longer sufficiently challenging to be worthy of their engagement.

Get excited and get the people they care about excited about their work too. A teacher's enthusiasm is contagious. Add the curiosity and excitement of their peers and families, and it will be hard for a student not to engage long enough to see what the excitement is all about. Plus, by building an environment focused on excitement for learning, students can start to believe that learning is exciting. Especially at the high school level, when so many students and teachers have forgotten to enjoy their work, modeling your own enjoyment is critical to showing your students that they can enjoy work too.

Outside of these considerations, you may need to examine socio-emotional issues affecting your students. Do you feel like you have a particularly hard time connecting with a group of students? Could you have internalized systemic messages about that group that affects how you perceive and interact with them? Consider how your resources include people like them, or how they don't, and what you can do to build community and safety in your classroom for everyone. Are there national or global issues affecting their community that you haven't acknowledged? We know representation matters, and it's easy to build our catalog of diverse stock images and clipart, but do your sources acknowledge the issues that affect them? Does your work include their voices and voices from their community? Per Maslow's Hierarchy of Needs, if your students are struggling to meet their basic or psychological needs, they will always struggle to reach their full potential with their work and learning[16]. This is why schools stock supply closets, run backpack programs, and employ counselors who work closely with social services. Trauma from individual experiences or on a large scale (like global pandemics or natural disasters) interrupts how students meet their psychological needs

---

16   Maslow, A.H. (1943). "A theory of human motivation". *Psychological Review.* 50(4): 370–96. CiteSeerX 10.1.1.334.7586. doi:10.1037/h0054346 – via psychclassics.yorku.ca.

and interfere with students' ability to respond to social triggers. Maybe the work you design or the tools you use for assessment need to incorporate some trauma-informed strategies.

Ultimately you are responsible for designing work that engages students. If they don't find your work engaging, the only thing you have control over is what you design next. You must build that relationship with your students day by day, task by task, where your focus is as much on persisting to create meaningful and valuable work, as it is for students to persist in creating meaningful and valuable products. We know that a model is a powerful tool for learning. Your students see the way you model work, and they will know how engaged you are. Perhaps you can return to the four factors of engagement at the start of the chapter and consider how you, as a teacher, can rediscover your own engagement.

BIG IDEAS

We know students are engaged in their work when they're interested enough to keep working on getting it right even when it is challenging or difficult. If we're not sure why or if students are engaged, the best way to find out is to ask! If students aren't engaged, then teachers need to build relationships with students to find out what kind of work is personally meaningful to them and how teachers can break down the barriers that prevent engagement.

Questions for Reflection

1. Think of a student you struggle to engage. What questions do you need to ask them to find out how to tailor the work to their needs and interests? What would make them want to "get it right," and not just get it done?
2. How could you find out from your students whether they thought a task you designed presented a "worthy challenge?" What would you expect them to say? How could you respond in such a way that more students would strongly agree that your work was a worthy challenge?
3. What makes your work interesting even when it's difficult?
4. What makes teaching personally meaningful for you? Why do you persist even when it's challenging or difficult? What does that tell you about student engagement?

WHAT'S NEXT?

IN WRITING THIS book, my goals are to coach you to:

- understand the work you design as a reflection of the design qualities that affect your students;
- measure your students' engagement and implement systems for reflection and redesign;
- craft "work": formative and summative assessments that have personal meaning to each of your students, and which also result in language mastery; and
- develop a hunger within you and your students to find power in language.

We studied what the design qualities are, how students can be moved by them, and how to design work that moves students. We compared the design qualities inherent in a variety of learning tasks and considered how modifying work to incorporate more design qualities can impact student achievement. We defined engagement and developed some formal and informal tools for determining how students engage with your work. We've talked about designing and assessing for proficiency and seen tools and resources for formative and summative assessment. We considered the power you have to guide students to find their voice in the world and become active and conscientious communicators. We've also reflected on poverty, class, and culture, and how your role as a world language teacher can equip our students with tools to rise above the challenges they face.

Now what? Each learner, each classroom, each day brings new challenges for teachers as designers. Certainly your accomplishments can be measured by test scores, or proficiency assessments, or competitive awards, but tomorrow will bring new challenges and new opportunities for action. Be intentional about reflecting on your role in the world and the legacy you leave in your students. You are their true model as a citizen in the world. Do you consider yourself to have a voice in a global community? Do you use it to make your community better? Students look to you to show them what it means to be a speaker of other languages. Show them that it's more than a proficiency score or a credit on a transcript or a Fiesta Funday.

I encourage you to ask yourself some critical questions as you move through your year:

- Did I make an effort to engage all students?
- What more could I do to reach those students who I have not engaged with my work?
- Is my classroom more than compliant?
- Have I engaged my students so thoroughly that they invest more of themselves than the task requires?
- Does this work have relevance outside of my classroom?
- Am I showing them every day that what they do matters? (Am I showing them every day that they matter?)

Working on the Work is a commitment to design and redesign that keeps student engagement for learning front and center. Commit yourself today to designing the best work to empower students with the communicative tools they need to make our world better.

An Afterword: Implications for Digital Learning

AS WE INCREASINGLY lead digital lives, our relationships, learning, and work will increasingly take place online. The COVID-19 pandemic school closures highlighted the ways in which we successfully transitioned to digital strategies and methods, but also exacerbated gaps in access and equity for many of our learners. In addition to the obvious challenges of moving from "face-to-face" to "face-to-device" learning, the crisis presented many students with challenges in meeting their physical and psychological needs while at home full time. We know schools provide so many more services than just teaching and learning, and that teaching and learning are supported by an army of dedicated support personnel. As you adapt to digital instruction, remember that many systems of support for learners may not be "fully online" to provide those scaffolds to student learning and readiness that you have come to expect in traditional classrooms.

As I watched my students, children, colleagues, and parent friends grapple with digital learning and reflected on how our work aligned with my own beliefs about learning by design, I feel confident that the design qualities are equally important elements of digital learning. Some world language teaching methodologies that depend on teacher-centered performance or require synchronous participation are so specific that they struggle to survive the transition to online instruction. It may not be feasible for you to engage your virtual learners synchronously and comprehensibly, but you can still provide culturally relevant comprehensible input and expect target language production. We know that simply digitizing existing work and pacing calendars is ineffective because independent digital learning happens at a different pace than classroom learning. I watched colleagues scan textbook exercises and drills, adapt them to editable slides, batch issue them to students, and then realize how much time it would take to review more than a hundred individual responses with twenty answers each. The students similarly struggled to figure out how to use editing tools they had never used and submit attached documents (turning a five-minute worksheet into a forty-minute endeavor), and then waited weeks for feedback. The work was not compelling, the product not meaningful, the organization challenging, on top of being completely oblivious to the students' abilities and time constraints with technology. By recognizing what elements engage learners, you can adapt to honor your learners' needs and deliver content meaningfully. I will briefly address each design quality from the lens of online instruction and some of the major takeaways to consider if your instruction will be partly or fully digital.

Protection from Adverse Consequences

When the in-person opportunity for practice and feedback was removed, my students still desired to be successful, even if the work didn't actually count for or against their grade. The opportunity to retake or continue practice before the graded assessment was important to their morale and motivation. For synchronous video events or recorded video, students were conscientious of their voice, appearance, and performance. During a class video conference, many opted to communicate via private message, rather than speak up or even message to the class chat. As a professional, I appreciated the freedom to "call in" to a meeting without having to livestream the background events of my life or home as well. For live presentation assignments, there are always several students who opt to pre-record their performance for the sake of meeting their own standards in presentation or dealing privately with their own anxieties. Consider the ways students are able to achieve and demonstrate success and make sure that all students are able to work without fear of punishment, embarrassment, or inadequacy.

Authenticity

My second-grade daughter's favorite part of the class video chat was the ten minutes before "class" where she could talk freely to her peers before class started. She desperately missed the social connections and affirmation that she had from her peers and teachers. If her teacher had asked students to digitally collaborate on an assignment, she would have been asking every day to get on the computer to talk to her partner. Instead, the longer she had to sit in front of a screen by herself, the more disheartened she became with her work. One of my students messaged me about halfway through the semester. He had only done a handful of assignments and was worried he was going to fail. He had taken a job to help support his family and was struggling to find time to catch up enough to pass. If he didn't keep his hours up at work, they would find someone else to fill the position. Another student with a 100 average who understood that pandemic classwork could not be used to lower her average opted not to do any assignments at all because the only way it could impact her grade was negatively. It would be nice if everybody felt they needed my work as much as I feel the need to share it, but I have to acknowledge that communicating in a second language is not an authentic motivator for all students all the time. The more I can consider what digital components do meet their needs, the more engagement I will nurture.

Choice

As we look toward a new school year with high levels of digitization, an easy way to honor choice is through flexibility with assignment format. Students have so many tools at their fingertips for digital work and products. Some can expertly manage those tools, and some don't even know they exist. Create an open-format assignment like "Create a brief biography of a famous person" and allow students to choose whether to make a video, a slideshow, a social media story, a narrative, or a website. While they have choice in terms of tools and content, as the designer, you set the standard and make clear what your expectations are for their product—both how they perform with language, and how thoroughly or creatively they provide content.

Product Focus

One of the biggest impacts on designing for digital classrooms is losing an audience for student work. Whether it was simply not having the time and place to share work with others or challenges of digital safety and privacy, students lose something by not being able to see their peers' work. They lost inspiration for what their work could be, they lost feedback for how they could improve, and they lost affirmation that they were doing good work.

As we consider what online education will look like, what our product (not just work) will be and who it will be for are important questions to ask. Even with the best of relationships, it is naive and arrogant for a teacher to believe that being the only audience and consumer of student work is enough to satisfy students. Teachers need to be creative and careful in how we showcase and incorporate student products in ways that are meaningful and extend beyond our own classrooms.

Clear and Compelling Standards

Just because we're adapting to a digital format doesn't mean the standards have changed. Of course it's simpler to design and assess discrete skills, and sometimes direct practice is necessary, but the more whole language we can use and expect, the more opportunities our students have to move towards proficiency. As you organize your digital instruction, consider what message the bold and highlighted titles communicate on the surface of your tasks. Is your work organized around a proficiency standard or around discrete skills? Are your objectives easy to identify? Are assessment standards easy to find and simply stated? Does the work take advantage of compelling digital resources from the digital world, or have you simply digitized an on-paper assignment? Is it easy for students to find scores and feedback, and are you able to return them in a timely fashion? The most frequent question I heard from students about online learning was, "Why do we have to do this?" Your digital work must have a clear purpose and a clear product. Your digital platform should not be redundant to in-person instruction. If your students could do the same activity in the classroom, consider how you can incorporate compelling digital tools and resources to create novel and compelling digital products.

Content and Substance

There is a delicate balance between how much time teachers and students are willing to dedicate to creating, completing, and assessing tasks, and doing high-quality, profound knowledge work. Particularly with varying internet access and time available to students, it is important that content be rich and simple to access. The more clicks or logins or downloads it takes to get through a task, the less likely it's getting done. For me, the best balance was to embed (link to) authentic digital sources and ask leveled questions about the source. Students are great at figuring information out and should be trusted and expected to look up the answers to their own questions. Incorporate target language broadcasts, tutorials, advertisements, websites, and info-graphics rich in authentic language, and target content of study through level-appropriate questions. Then, coax students to make meaning from the big picture, and to dig deeper for details. Not only do they develop language skills, but they begin to develop universal skills like reading charts and maps or checking titles and bold or italicized words for big ideas. One of the benefits of embedding digital content is the additional authentic connection to current life. Many of the resources I used during COVID closures were pandemic-related content that addressed our classroom thematic unit and structures. For example, in a unit about giving health commands, I found a target language infographic about hand washing. In a unit about community leaders, I found a target language news segment about community leaders organizing a local relief effort. As I tell my students, they don't have to understand every word, they just have to understand enough to answer the questions, which are intentionally formatted to recycle studied content and structures. The balance is found in using authentic whole language sources with targeted student responses to help students bring content into focus.

Organization of Knowledge

One of my biggest frustrations is trying to efficiently navigate poorly organized information. If the answers are hard to find or time-consuming to access, students will stop looking or look elsewhere. Keeping your content neat and clearly organized will facilitate your students' work. As an added bonus, it makes you appear more professional and builds positive relationships because your organization is considerate of students' time and needs. Digital learners may be juggling numerous work platforms, tools, expectations, and deadlines, so the more you can streamline yours for students, the more you ease the burden that your work places on them, and the more they can focus on the work itself.

Affirmation

In the course of in-person learning, students receive affirmation from peers, teachers, and staff on an ongoing basis throughout the day. With digital learning, feedback is limited to graded assignments and may be partially automated. It is important to continue to offer "digital models" that help students know what good work looks like, to personally and publicly celebrate student achievement, either in individual feedback on tasks or through public recognition during class meetings or on a class "celebration wall" in their online platform. As an added source of affirmation, if you share student accomplishments (safely) to digital bulletin boards or wow walls where parents can share in celebrating student success, you build community affirmation into your students' engagement.

Affiliation

There are many benefits to using digital workspaces for collaborative work. Many even have added accountability features that can reveal what students have contributed and in what ways. Because many young people are already communicating through technology, opening doors for digital collaboration gives them an opportunity to bring some of their digital talents into academia and make many of their social media skills relevant to learning. Online learning is an opportunity to make digital collaboration mainstream in our classrooms in meaningful and necessary ways. By moving collaboration to the cloud, we also increase opportunities to build student familiarity with digital resources and references in ways that support special needs and equip learners that may not have support with digital competency at home.

Novelty and Variety

Technological innovation is at once amazing and overwhelming. I have learned to temper my excitement over novel tech tools and tips for the sake of my less tech-savvy colleagues and students by focusing on those tools that are affordable (free), schoolhouse filter-friendly, and which don't require much set-up or explanation. Incorporating digital tools into instruction and assessment is fantastic when it's under my control, but the time and effort it might take some learners to navigate is sometimes more of a deterrent than a resource. In terms of world language, the clear benefit comes from the wide world of digital target language content literally at our fingertips. Just as we lead learners to discover content in the classroom, so too do we cultivate digital content in ways that make it accessible for students. Many might otherwise never access target language content, while others are thrilled to have their interests and digital lives represented in the classroom. Further, digital work is an opportunity to break with classroom habits and ways of doing things—to refresh formats and acknowledge other ways of learning and producing. This variety enhances the spectrum that you can offer students and use to engage them in the work you design.

Acknowledgments

I must start by thanking the Professional Association of Georgia Educators (PAGE) for giving me opportunities for learning and leadership and empowering me to pursue my dreams. The training and mentorship I had under the Schlechty Center team, specifically the influence of Annissa Roland and Deanna Howard, gave me a philosophical foundation that guides my understanding of the work we do, how we do it, and why. I am particularly thankful to Annissa for making space for my own critical reflection and leading me to see the power of my voice and that of my students.

To those who read my work and encouraged me to keep going— Steve McCammon, George Thompson, Meg Thornton, Lisa Shepard, Kara Parker, Katy Rosenbaum, Anne Stucke, Nadeen Pagano, colleagues, friends —thank you. To my HoCo and GCSU families, thank you for loving me and encouraging me.

Dr. Coia, you have been one of the earliest and most lasting influences on my formation as an educator. I am grateful for your encouragement and for always asking questions that pushed the boundaries of my thinking.

David Reynolds, your friendship, commentary, and coaxing have been an ongoing motivation for me for which I am exceptionally grateful. I appreciate the way you have walked with me on this journey, how you have listened to my story, and how you have gifted me your time, wisdom, and affirmation.

Dear Caroline, thanks for taking a chance on me and blessing me with your incredible talent. Mom, thank you for making me rewrite all those high school essays even through my adolescent frustration. You were right; it really was worth it, and it made me into the writer I am today. Kenneth, thanks for getting excited with me, being patient with me, and making room for me to dedicate myself to my passions and projects. To my children, biological or borrowed for a year or two at a time, thank you for inspiring me, loving me, challenging me, helping me learn and unlearn how to serve you, and for always expecting my best.

About the Author

Megan Golden is in her second decade teaching Spanish in middle Georgia public high schools. Her classroom serves students across academic, economic, linguistic, and ethnic spectra. She started her career with Foreign Language Teaching Certification and a BA in Spanish from Agnes Scott College in Atlanta and is working toward an EdD in Curriculum & Instruction at Georgia College & State University. Her philosophy and practice are deeply shaped by her training with the Schlechty Center and its framework for design and engagement. She grew up near Buford Highway and Spaghetti Junction, has traveled in five countries, and can't wait to visit more. She has a passion for Latin American literature and social justice.

www.ingramcontent.com/pod-product-compliance
Lightning Source LLC
Chambersburg PA
CBHW070720130626
46553CB00005B/2070